Stoneflies

Stoneflies

BY CARL RICHARDS
DOUG SWISHER
FRED ARBONA, JR.

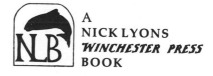

A
NICK LYONS
WINCHESTER PRESS
BOOK

Books by Doug Swisher and Carl Richards

Selective Trout
Fly-Fishing Strategy
Tying the Swisher/Richards Flies

By Fred Arbona, Jr.

Mayflies, the Angler, and the Trout

Designed by Ruth Kolbert
Composition by Publishers Phototype, Inc., Carlstadt, N.J.
PRINTED IN THE UNITED STATES OF AMERICA

Library of Congress Cataloging in Publication Data

Richards, Carl, 1933-
  Stoneflies.
  A Nick Lyons/Winchester Press Book.
  Bibliography, p. 187.
  Includes index.
  1. Stoneflies. 2. Fly Fishing. 3. Flies, artificial.
I. Swisher, Doug, joint author.
II. Arbona, Jr., Fred, joint author.
III. Title.
SH456.R555   799.1'2   80-18317
ISBN 0-87691-327-3

Nick Lyons Books
is a division of
BENN BROTHERS, INC.,
212 Fifth Avenue
New York, N.Y. 10010

Contents

ACKNOWLEDGMENTS

We would especially like to thank the following people for their generous help with this book:

Dr. J. Frederic Oswalt, who did much of the photography with his collection of Hasselblads, is a master of photography and fly tying; he took the excellent color transparencies of the artificial flies, and some of the blonde nymphs are his creation. His help was greatly appreciated.

Dr. Richard Baumann of the Department of Zoology, Brigham Young University, and author of *The Stoneflies of the Rocky Mountains.* He is one of the world's leading experts of Plecoptera and his help was invaluable to us.

Mike Lawson—one of the greatest professional fly tyers in the world. Many of the stonefly patterns in this book were created by Mike. He is the owner of Henry's Fork Anglers, located on the banks of the Snake River, in Last Chance, Idaho. He is as great an angler as he is a fly tyer.

Poul Jorgensen—author of many great fly-tying works and of course a superb tyer. He created the two Jorgensen nymphs, the Big Black and Big Golden patterns, and the Streaker Atlantic salmon flies.

Dave Whitlock—master fishing artist. We thank him for tying some of the Atlantic salmon stonefly patterns used in this book.

Bill Styler for his sketches of casting positions in Chapter Five, and for his line sketches in Chapter Seven.

Steve Lavely for various black-and-white photographs of artificials and Ron Falk for tying them.

Cyndy De Mann—for the hours she spent typing and deciphering our handwriting.

The jacket and chapter-opening art were done by Jim Marc, Jr. The line drawings for Chapters Two, Three, and Four were done by Fred Arbona, Jr. The line drawings for Appendix II were done by Carl Richards.

Introduction

Masses of black clouds swept across the slate-gray sky. It was an unseasonably warm day in early March, yet there was still snow along the trout stream's banks, and nothing much was expected to hatch. We were surprised, however, when rather large, slim, black forms appeared, literally skipping across the water's surface toward shore. Although we saw few rises, many flashing trout became noticeable in the deep runs, the flashes indicating that the trout were feeding heavily on active nymphs. On close observation we found a stonefly emergence and simultaneous egg-laying flight in progress. The adults were dive-bombing from high over the river, hitting the surface of the water in the egg-laying process, then "running" to shore over the stream's surface. Under the surface, active nymphs were crawling to shore, where they would later molt into adults. Great brown trout were feeding occasionally on the egg-laying adults, but more often on the shoreward-migrating immature forms.

On top of the other surprises, this was a smooth, quiet, limestone river, not the typically fast, cold, boulder-filled freestone river that is normally associated with stoneflies. It was a full six weeks before the earliest Hendricksons could be expected and at least three weeks before the small, early-season Blue-Winged Olives *(Baetis vagans)* would be seen. Yet there we had brown and brook trout feeding on comparatively large stoneflies. We checked the stomach contents of the fish we landed with stomach pumps, and we found the fish filled with #14, brownish-black stonefly nymphs, many of which were still alive. We counted few adults.

This and other similar incidents peaked our curiosity enough to begin a study of the much-neglected yet extremely important aquatic-insect order Plecoptera, or stoneflies.

It soon became obvious that there was much we did not know, understand or appreciate about stoneflies, and that a great deal of erroneous information about them has been written and perpetuated. First, and perhaps most important, the Plecoptera are a vastly more important food source for fish than has been generally recognized. Second, no species of stoneflies emerges from the water and then flies to shore, as has been reported by fishing writers. All the nymphs crawl out to molt on land. Third, all families of stoneflies are an extremely valuable food source, not only during the egg-laying flight (or spinner fall) but also when the mature nymphs migrate from deep riffles to shore. In fact, on thousands of streams (probably most of our North American trout streams) stonefly nymphs and adults are either the primary or secondary food source for trout, easily surpassing both mayflies and caddisflies in importance as a food source.

Rivers in all parts of the country, even the slower flows, usually have at least four stonefly species that create flush nymphal migrations or egg-laying flights, and the rapid-flowing streams have many more. At these times—during the migration of the nymphs and the egg-laying of the adults—the Plecoptera are as important as any mayfly in creating great match-the-hatch fishing to rising trout. In many areas the majority of dry-fly activity is due to the Plecoptera.

This study of the stoneflies was difficult, but it became necessary because they have truly been an understudied and a misunderstood group of insects. Little has been written about them, and much that has been written is incomplete, dead wrong, or thirty years out of date according to the discoveries of modern entomologists.

Many times we found that when we were trying to match the hatch at a time we expected a particular mayfly or caddisfly, we were completely surprised by unexpected stonefly activity. This activity was, to say the least, baffling, and it usually found us without a good imitation.

One example occurred a few years ago, in June, on the main stream of Michigan's Au Sable above Stephan Bridge. This is in the flies-only water, and we thought we would be evening fishing to the Pale Evening Dun *(Ephemerella dorothea)* and were quite well prepared to match the emerging nymph, the dun, and the spinner. Instead we were confronted with a small, yellow-sulphur stonefly at dusk, for which we had nothing in our fly boxes that was close in appearance. On another occasion, just last spring, on a slow, smooth, gravel-bottom stream in northern Idaho, at 10

A.M. rainbows were rising—but not to the expected Pale Morning Duns. Instead it was to a 10mm long, tannish-yellow stonefly with a reddish cast to the body. This was anything but traditional stonefly water. Even so, we had purchased a few Mormon Girls, which are stonefly imitations, in the local fly shop, so we had some flies—after all, we were in the West, which is considered stonefly country. However, we were still unprepared for *this specific* stonefly, because our artificals were the wrong size. We had over-stuffed boxes of caddisfly imitations, a box of nymphs, and a very large box for mayfly patterns—all three selections specifically for this one river in the last two weeks of June. But we were not equipped to match this particular Plecoptera, and so we went fishless for a while.

As our investigation into the Plecoptera progressed we found that stonefly nymphs do not necessarily or even usually require stones for habitat, nor do all species need fast water, nor do they need particularly cold and clear water. In fact, most slow, quiet streams, such as the spring creeks and limestoners, which are usually considered mayfly streams, harbor myriad Plecoptera of various species. Stoneflies are actually a wonderfully adaptive order of insects and can be found in almost every type of aquatic ecosystem. It is, of course, true that stoneflies thrive in extremely fast, cold, tumbling mountain rivers and streams, where they are most abundant, sometimes to the exclusion of most other types of insects. In these locales they are the primary food source for trout and other fish. Many other stonefly types, however, have adapted to slower, more placid streams, and some species are even found in semitropical locales.

Unlike the Ephemeroptera, or mayflies, and Trichoptera, or caddisflies, there is a considerable winter fauna of Plecoptera that covers virtually the entire area in which trout are found. These small, black, winter stoneflies provide much-needed nourishment to fish in the cold months, when little else is available. Many anglers have the mistaken idea that trout do not feed in the winter. This is definitely not true. They do considerable feeding in cold weather, though admittedly not as much as they do in May or June when the metabolism of the fish is at its peak. The winter stoneflies (along with Midges) probably provide the bulk of insect food to trout in the cold months, even in the slow rivers.

In the early spring the rich, fast rivers explode with stonefly activity. A sample of the bottom of such a river will show a great number and variety of Plecoptera. And regular stonefly emergences also occur throughout the summer months on many waters.

A few years ago, we spent some time in the Idaho-Montana-Wyoming area fishing the rivers and studying the insects. We were staying at Island Park, Idaho, and fishing Henrys Fork of the Snake River. This was our home base, and from there we made short trips in every direction to different types of rivers.

The difference in the content of the water's biomass available to fish in such rivers as the Henrys Fork and other spring creeks and some of the faster freestone streams, such as the Madison and the Big Hole, was almost unbelievable. While the Henrys Fork had many stoneflies, by far the greatest amount of food by weight were the mayfly nymphs and caddisfly larvae of all sizes. The first time we seined the Madison the difference was astounding. By far the greatest amount of food by weight were stonefly nymphs: gigantic ones, medium-size ones, small ones, and tiny ones. To be sure, there were some mayfly nymphs in the Madison, but mostly they were rather small, and by far the greatest number of species were stoneflies.

The importance of stoneflies as a fish food in fast-water streams, such as the Madison, the Big Hole, New York's Ausable and the Beaverkill, is obvious. In streams such as these, stoneflies are often the primary or secondary food source. Since some species of stoneflies live two or three years as nymphs, and since many species emerge in the winter, there are always nymphs present and available for fish to eat. We have found that most streams that are normally considered limestone or spring creeks have four or five major stonefly emergences during the year. Of course, stoneflies on these gentle rivers are not usually as important as mayflies or caddisflies; however, during the flush emergences of stoneflies, they are fed on exclusively—and especially on these streams one must have a good imitation and know the insect's habits to be successful. There are over 461 species of stoneflies north of Mexico, and stoneflies are found in virtually all productive trout streams. Many species have adapted to slow-flowing, warm-water streams in the South and Midwest. Stoneflies are found almost everywhere, even along the stony shorelines of some of our colder lakes.

After experiencing many instances of flush hatches and selectively rising trout and finding ourselves completely unprepared, we decided to continue our investigation and make a thorough study of the stoneflies. For us the results are not only startling but also rewarding. When we understood the Plecoptera we found it possible and necessary to break down the rather bewildering scientific keys and to classify the stoneflies into what could be called fisherman's terms. Only six major types of Plecoptera are really present for our purposes. This brings the 461-plus species down to a manageable, understandable level. Here is our fisherman's classification:

WINTER STONEFLIES

1. The Tiny Winter Blacks (6mm long, blackish)
2. The Early Black Stones and Brown Stones (12mm long, brown and black)

SPRING STONEFLIES

3. The Salmon Flies (40mm long, brownish black with orange thorax)

SUMMER STONEFLIES

4. The Big Goldens (25mm long, brownish yellow)
5. The Medium Brown Stones (14–23mm long, medium brown)
6. The Little Yellows and Greens (10mm long, pale yellow or olive green)

Because each type has a particular season, size, and color, we have been able to devise a simple, prototypical series of nymph and adult imitations for our fly boxes that will match virtually any stonefly one may encounter in this country. One or two sizes in a certain color combination can be representative of many species. For example, the little yellows and greens of summer, which later in the book we refer to collectively as the Chloroperlidae (the late-summer fauna), actually include the genera *Alloperla, Paraperla, Hastaperla, Chloroperl,* and some others. But two color types in two color sizes adequately imitate the Chloroperlidae—in this instance that includes ten genera and fifty-seven species. The same is true of the other five main types listed above, so we have greatly reduced the number and complexity of the patterns required to imitate this large and complex order of trout-stream insects realistically.

In the chapters that follow, we find it best to give the reader the common names and scientific designations of the most important species. We also feel that it would be practical to take certain liberties in the scientific classifications of certain stoneflies. Lately, many changes have been proposed by the Europeans concerning the establishment of a multitude of genera for the placement of distinct species that are now classified collectively under families. We choose not to follow their more complex designations. They appear to be more dependent on taxonomic differences than consideration to the common biology exhibited by certain species of natural groups. Thus, our classifications follow that of Dr. W. E. Ricker (1952). For the sake of brevity and out of consideration for the reader, we will refer to certain types by a single, scientific name. Thus, the family Capniidae, composed of genera *Allocapnia, Capnia,* and *Paracapnia,* will simply be referred to as the *Capnia.* However, with the hope of establishing a useful and precise reference for future angling texts on stoneflies, we will be specific as to the species that make up the hatches of stoneflies that anglers will encounter 90 percent of the time they are on the stream. Later, in Appendix Two, a list of the most complete, though more complex, references will be included for those who wish to become better aquainted with the specific species and their up–to–date classifications.

CHAPTER ONE

A Streamside Introduction to Stoneflies

MOST ANGLERS' EXPERIENCE WITH STONEFLIES HAS BEEN MAINLY CONFINED TO imitating the largest forms of the insect. Stoneflies such as the salmon flies and the big goldens are well known to many anglers. However, the importance of many other species, more numerous though smaller in size, is often overlooked. These smaller species can create great selective rises of trout and are often more important than the very large Plecoptera.

Of the principal types of aquatic insects found in trout streams, stoneflies have been given the least space in angling literature. While publications dealing mainly with fly-tying have been considerably more generous to this order of insects, it is also important for the angler to know the times of the year that stoneflies are of greatest importance, times of the day they can be expected to emerge, how to fish most successfully during their emergence and mating flight, and when and why a stonefly imitation can be used during nonhatch periods.

The existing void is not the result of conscious neglect on the part of angling authors. They don't necessarily feel that stoneflies, in general, merit only superficial treatment. Stoneflies are neglected because they are secretive insects and do not lend themselves to comfortable study. All stoneflies, however, reveal their presence in trout streams by their peculiar manner of emergence; the nymphs crawl out of the water before molting into the winged adult form. Evidence of such nymph-to-adult transition is visible in the form of large numbers of discarded shucks along the banks of a stream. Little information is available on the underwater feeding that takes place when trout prey upon the shoreward-migrating nymphs. Merely seeing the shucks does not tell the fisherman the time of day the actual emergence occurred or when the adults will return to the stream and again be available to the trout. But these are important concerns to the fly fisherman and we will cover these topics in this chapter so the reader can place himself in the right spot at the right time throughout the season.

Fly-fishing encompasses many philosophies of approach. No two fly fishermen, fishing in the same stream at the same time, will fish for trout in exactly the same fashion; the approach to the sport is quite personal. Perhaps no other approach, however, is more interesting and rewarding than that of recognizing and familiarizing oneself with the insect that one is supposed to be representing. The knowledge gained by categorizing insects and studying a stream will undoubtedly lead to better presentation of the fly. In this way the angler can mimic the movements and behavior of the natural enough to cause the trout to take the artificial as frequently and as confidently as it would the real thing. We believe that if the angler knows how the insect behaves, he will be better prepared to fish its imitation. This belief is based on streamside results and not armchair logic. Because of this belief, in this chapter we will concentrate on the naturals, while in following chapters we will concentrate on the exact presentation and the few artificials required to succeed with selective trout when they are feeding on stoneflies.

We will not exaggerate the importance of stoneflies as a food source for trout at the expense of other important aquatic insects that they share their environment with. These other insects include, primarily, mayflies, caddisflies, and midges. As with other types of insects, stoneflies have their own niche in the trout stream and thus become exceedingly significant during specific times of the season and of the day. Circumstances sometimes cause their significance to the trout and the angler to be preempted by other insects, as when concentrated hatches of these other types appear and carpet the water. But the different insect orders are not in conflict; interestingly enough, they complement each other, both to the trout's and the fisherman's point of view.

We will not assume that the reader already knows what to look for in order to make streamside differentiations between the most common types of trout-stream insects. To make it easier for the angler we will briefly tell what to look for.

Principal Aquatic Insects Found in Most Trout Streams

In the great majority of trout waters mayflies, caddisflies, midges, and stoneflies are forced to exist with one another, and they exhibit spacial or temporal relations to each other, either in the time of the year they become most active or the time of the day they hatch.

Mayflies (order Ephemeroptera) are the best known of all the types of insects discussed here. Their high esteem is due partly to the fact that the majority of their hatches take place during the most comfortable times of the year to fish. They hatch daily from midmorning until dusk. Their hatches are customarily comprised of a single species emerging in one great concentration. These are perhaps the most intriguing and demanding hatches of the season, often prompting trout to feed on the surface quite selectively. Mayflies are delicate and beautiful insects in their dun and spinner stages and have been the subject of angling writers more often than any other type included here.

The overall importance of mayflies to the angler must be mentioned with certain reservations, however. Their greatest populations are confined to slow- to medium-flowing trout streams, especially those choked with aquatic vegetation; these latter streams are waters in which they dominate almost exclusively. Moreover, their activity peaks between spring and midsummer, with some species continuing to hatch until fall.

Streamside recognition of the mayfly's adult stages is relatively easy.

The mayfly has a pair of large wings held in an upright position, or spread-eagle position (after mating and egg laying). Most species have a second pair of inconspicuous wings behind the larger pair. The subaquatic or nymphal stage has but one pair of visible wing pads (or cases), and the great majority of mayfly species has three tails (there are only three exceptions).

Caddisflies (order Trichoptera) also produce many excellent hatches throughout the season. They are very important in trout streams in certain areas of the country, though they have not received the same degree of attention from anglers as the mayflies have.

Found in a wide diversity of trout waters, caddisflies achieve their most concentrated hatches in medium- to fast-running trout streams. The best caddisfly activity takes place somewhat later than that of mayflies, mainly during summer and early fall. Daily hatches are comparatively sporadic when compared to those of the mayflies. However, the hatches of the more important forms of caddisflies can be expected to begin at approximately the same date and time every year.

The adult phase of the caddisfly, as in the case of the other three insect types discussed here, constitutes a short period of the total life cycle. They differ from stoneflies and mayflies in that they possess two pair of tentlike wings that entirely covers the abdomen (rear half of the body). Subaquatic stages are apparent in two forms: house-building and free-living. The first type is larvae that make ingenious use of available material found in the bottom of the trout stream. With this material they construct a case, or house, in which to spend the larval stage. Free-living forms, such as the common *Hydropsyche,* do not spend the stage within the protection of an encasement; rather, they crawl about unprotected.

Midges (order Diptera), or true flies, are small insects, and their importance in trout streams is twofold: food for other aquatic insects and food for trout. They are important to anglers when trout consume emerging pupae or the adults in great numbers. Their hatches, although hard to detect, are more significant in many trout waters than most anglers realize, especially during the spring. Their greatest importance is in slow-moving spring creeks and in cold lakes. The slow-moving spring-fed streams are most common in the high-altitude areas of the western mountains.

Adult Diptera are easily recognized by their small size and a single pair of wings that is atop the abdomen. They usually belong to either the Simulidae type (the annoying biting flies) or the cold-water-inhabiting Chironomidae.

Stoneflies (order Plecoptera), perhaps by sheer muscle, large size, and carnivorous nature, occupy an important niche in trout waters. They are the principal reason that the populations of the little midges are kept in control, even though they compete with the mayflies and the caddisflies for their food. Like other types, stoneflies prefer certain times of the year for hatching. Their first hatches begin during January and February, well in advance of those of mayflies and caddisflies, and they continue to emerge until late summer.

Adult stoneflies can be found along the banks of a stream in a wide variety of sizes, ranging from 5 to 40mm long (#20 to #2 hooks) throughout the season. All have wings that lie flat over the abdomen, with one exception: the little *Leuctras.* These flies have wings rolled around their bodies, giving them such a thin shape that they have earned the name "needle flies." All stonefly nymphs have two tails and are easily distinguished from caddisfly larvae by general configuration and from the three-tailed mayfly nymphs (with the exception of the two-tailed nymphs of *Epeorus, Pseudocloeon* and certain species of *Baetis*). Moreover, the stonefly nymphs also have a *double* set of wing pads rather than the single visible wing pad found on mayfly nymphs.

Stonefly Habitat

Cool-running streams and cold lakes, the same aquatic stations occupied by trout, support the greatest populations of stoneflies. These waters usually consist of smooth-faced rocks and boulders, where stonefly nymphs and nymphs of other aquatic insects crawl along the bottom to escape

The Brodheads—fine eastern stonefly water

Even placid rivers and spring creeks (like those on this and the following page) have good stonefly hatches.

their natural enemies. They also gain access to the decaying vegetable and animal matter pinched between such rocks. But by no means is the stoneflies' distribution confined to rocky-bottom trout waters. Like mayflies and caddisflies, they can also be found in heavily silted stretches that are unsuitable for trout. Thus, the common belief that stoneflies are only found in extremely cold water and fast-flowing streams and are confined to rocky-bottom environments is erroneous. This suggests that their common name is really a misnomer.

Nonhatch Periods

Strictly from a biological point of view (but of great importance to the fly fisher) stoneflies are extremely important insects because they convert trash and vegetation into trout food, namely themselves. Because of their size, stoneflies often become more important than mayflies or caddisflies. This is specifically the case during nonhatch periods.

Many stoneflies require a full year to reach maturity, though the larger types need a second or even a third year to complete their growth. Since the larger types will attain half their growth during their "off year," they will be available to the trout in sizes approximating ¾ to 1 inch in length. In most cases this makes them the largest insects available to the trout at any time of the season. Their size ensures that they are a popular morsel for good-size trout year-round. This is especially true when no other insects are emerging.

The popular notion that pattern selection during nonhatch periods should follow the "bigger-the-better" rule is in many respects true. As trout grow larger they prefer larger prey. It may be surmised that if trout had an uninhibited free choice, the bigger brutes would feed upon the smaller members of their own kind continually. But small trout are often elusive, so bigger trout have to settle for the next best thing around: large stoneflies. The choice by trout during nonhatch periods goes according to the most *sizable* and *available* prey.

It may sound at first quite surprising that *selectivity can and does occur during nonhatch periods.* The scientist calls this the "available factor," which mathematically demonstrates the trout's preference for the largest and most available insect forms. These insects constitute a greater percentage of the stomach contents of trout. Our own observations lead us to believe that high ratios of selection to stonefly nymphs occur during nonhatch periods for a number of reasons. First, most are large in size and cannot help advertising themselves when drifting in the undercurrents. Second, they are

perpetually being dislodged from their protective lairs. Third, they must undergo concentrated migrations toward the banks of a stream before their actual emergence.

Equally significant, migrating fish, such as salmon and steelhead, also exhibit a marked preference for the larger stonefly types. We have put this knowledge to good use and have often had good success with stonefly imitations when fishing unfamiliar steelhead and salmon waters that are devoid of any surface activity.

It has also become apparent on numerous occasions that stoneflies come in different types and sizes at certain times of the season. We've discovered that using an imitation that approximates the basic size and shape of the insect that should be the most active at that time of the year often worked better than simply fishing with the largest stonefly patterns in our fly boxes.

Hatch Periods

Most fly fishermen prefer to fish during a hatch. At such times the trout are prompted to rise to floating naturals that ride the surface of the water. At certain times of the day and year, stoneflies can produce this hatch scenario for the angler. As a rule, they will produce significant hatches during the cold months of January, February, and March. Many of their winter flush emergences are confined to small and medium-size freestone streams and rivers. This winter emergence falls outside the legal fishing season in many states, not to mention outside the enthusiasm of the many anglers who are unwilling to venture out to the streams so early in the year. Moreover, the metabolism of the trout does not peak until the water temperature reaches the 50-degree mark.

Springtime is the season to begin fly-fishing earnestly. It marks the emergence of legions of eager anglers trekking toward their local rivers. They will probably begin the season with well-oiled reels, clean fly lines, exuberant spirits and high hopes for the coming season. The winter stoneflies that continue to emerge into spring will unknowingly play an important role in satisfying their high expectations. In the East and Midwest the seasonally waning tiny winter blacks and early brown stones will be most effective. In the West, because of the effects of the higher altitudes, the little winter stoneflies will still be emerging abundantly, with the early brown stones not peaking until late April or May. Both of the winter types will eventually disappear for the season, and the trout waters will be dominated by much larger stoneflies, (such as the *Pteronarcys,* or salmon fly.) These, in turn, will be succeeded by the nocturnal stoneflies of summer.

The summer stonefly activity is brought about by three types, the big goldens, medium browns, and the little yellows and greens. These flies exhibit a strong tendency to emerge and become most active between late afternoon and early morning. Hence, their hatches complement the daytime hatches of the mayflies and caddisflies. Night anglers and early-rising anglers will benefit from this "off-hours" activity. This is fortunate for those anglers because big browns like to feed at night.

There are, however, many notable and important summer stoneflies that are morning and dusk emergers. We will emphasize these types in Chapter Four. Many of the stoneflies' impressive hatches and egg-laying activities have gone largely unnoticed by anglers. Because of increasing competition between anglers and canoeists, campers and wanderers, these "off-hours" stonefly activities will probably gain importance in the future for fly fishers who are looking for solitude.

Seasonal Emergences of Stoneflies

Stoneflies display certain unmistakable transformations in appearance and streamside habits as the season progresses. Here we will discuss only those changes that are relevant to fly-fishing. It should be noted that our splitting of the stoneflies into two types here, "winter-spring" and "summer," are categories that we choose to give them for the purposes of convenience and understanding for the reader in this chapter. In later chapters we divide them into three groups, winter, spring, and summer, for more specific consideration.

WINTER-SPRING STONEFLIES

The winter-spring stoneflies are composed of three types. The first begin to emerge in January and will continue doing so through April and

A stonefly extruding eggs

even May in some locales. They are tiny (4–7mm) and dark, thus we have named them tiny winter blacks. These tiny winter forms are found throughout the country. Late-winter emergers are abundant and are considerably larger in size (10–15mm). A more appropriate common name for them is early black stones (*Taeniopteryx*), of importance only in eastern and midwestern waters. The last to emerge are the early brown stones (*Brachypteras*), whose geographical range encompasses the entire country. Their growth is continued well into late spring, either April, May, or June, depending on the area, when the hatches of the gigantic salmon flies (*Pteronarcys*) make their seasonal debut. These are the largest stoneflies (32–40 mm), and for that matter the largest aquatic insects in North American waters. They are abundant and significant in western waters. All winter-spring types exhibit certain parallel characteristics. Of greatest relevance to the fly fisher is that they are all midday emergers and that their adult forms can live for three or four weeks after the actual emergence.

Stoneflies must leave their aquatic habitat in order for the nymph-to-adult metamorphosis to take place. The cycle's completion is dependent not only on the nymphs reaching the rocks or logs along the margin of the stream, but on the ability of the adults to break the nymphal shucks in order to escape. Hardening of the nymphal shuck, caused either by the direct sun or exceedingly dry, hot air, can prove fatal. However, bright sunny days of winter and spring seem ideal for the midday emergence of stoneflies. It is at such times that the tiny winter blacks, early black stones, and early brown stones will come out of the water. The salmon flies, which emerge during spring and even into early summer in many areas, exercise more caution. In the West, due to the cooler temperatures of the higher elevations, *Pteronarcys,* as do their seasonal predecessors, continue to emerge at midday. Their best hatches are during overcast days that afford them some protection from the sun. Eastern specimens of this stonefly, the *Pteronarcys dorsata*, which emerge from the latter part of April until early June, hatch both earlier and later in the day during the second half of their seasonal cycle. Their hatches at such times are missed by most anglers who are not accustomed to fishing before eight A.M. or after dusk.

After actual emergence takes place, winter-spring stoneflies demonstrate the remarkable ability to live in the adult stage up to four weeks before completing the mating-ovipositing phase of the life cycle. This is because the adults are able to feed on the algae growth on rocks, bark, and streamside vegetation. Some stonefly adults are nonfeeders. Encountering these stoneflies at streamside usually means that the hatching is taking place in the stream nearby. However, it is also possible that the hatch is currently located well upstream from where they are found.

Stonefly hatches move upstream because each species must experience a certain number of days with water temperatures that are conducive to growth (between 35 and 65 degrees) in order to hatch. This first occurs in the lowest sections of a river system, farthest from the cold headwaters.

The water in these lower sections has been exposed longer to the warming rays of the sun. Thus, the hatches of a particular species will first appear in the lower reaches and progressively move upstream. In some cases, it will require up to a month and a half to complete the emergence cycle in a particular river. No better example exists than that of the salmon-fly hatches in western waters. They travel upstream approximately four or five miles a day.

That winter-spring stoneflies can exist for weeks after their emergence and the hatches move upstream should warn the angler that the mere presence of adults along the stream does not mean that the hatches are still taking place. If the adults are already copulating, it is usually an indication that the hatch may have expired, and the egg-laying activity of the adults will now be of most concern to the angler.

The summer stoneflies are also composed of three principal types. The first emergences are by what is probably the most important stonefly to the fly fisher, the big golden. Its seasonal occurrences begin in the wake of the slightly larger salmon fly. Its proportions range from 22 to 28mm, but it is the big golden's abundance in most trout streams that makes it so significant. The smaller and paler medium brown is a second summer stonefly that appears from June to early August. The third type, the little yellow and green, is at its best during August, September, and even October, although many species appear in late May, June, and July.

Stoneflies, then, when considering the entire year, will peak in size of the insect with the emergences of the spring hatches of the salmon flies, and then begin to reverse the process toward winter. In coloration, they get paler as the season progresses.

The three summer types also exhibit certain parallel traits. In contrast to the winter-spring stoneflies, they emerge between early evening and the morning hours. The adults live for only a short time, three to five days. The hot temperatures of summer discourage their hatches from taking place during the day, so most species hatch during the cooler times of the day, and many hatch at night. The fact that the adults live briefly would imply that when an angler encounters them in the vegetation along the stream, he can expect their actual emergences still to be occurring nearby in the stream.

It is interesting to note that many summer stoneflies have short, nonfunctional wings in the adult stage and that the females emerge with already developed eggs. Apparently, nature wants to ensure that they do not venture too far from their point of origin. This facilitates the quick completion of the mating-fertilization-ovipositing processes of the life cycle and the greatest chance for survival of the species.

So far we have made many generalizations concerning the eastern, midwestern, and western stoneflies as to the domination of certain types and to specific times of the day and year they emerge. The accompanying charts summarize this information.

EMERGENCE TABLE FOR MIDWEST AND EAST

WINTER-SPRING

		JANUARY	FEBRUARY	MARCH	APRIL	MAY	JUNE	JULY	AUGUST	SEPTEMBER	OCTOBER
	Midnight										
	8 P.M.										
	4 P.M.										
	NOON										
	8 A.M.										
	4 A.M.										

THE TINY WINTER BLACKS
(Allocapnia granulata)
(Allocapnia vivipara)
(Paracapnia angulata)
(Nemoura albidipennis)

EASTERN SALMON FLY — 2

EARLY BLACK STONE
(Taeniopteryx nivalis)

EARLY BLACK/BROWN STONE — 1

EARLY BROWN STONE
(Brachyptera fasciata)

TINY WINTER BLACKS — 1

TINY WINTER BLACKS

EASTERN SALMON FLY
(Pteronarcys dorsata)

EASTERN SALMON FLY — 2

SUMMER

		JANUARY	FEBRUARY	MARCH	APRIL	MAY	JUNE	JULY	AUGUST	SEPTEMBER	OCTOBER
	Midnight										
	8 P.M.										
	4 P.M.										
	NOON										
	8 A.M.										
	4 A.M.										

THE BIG GOLDENS
(Phasganophora capitata)
(Acroneuria lycorias)
(Paragnetina media)

BIG GOLDENS — 2

THE MEDIUM BROWNS
(Isogenus decisus)
(Isoperla signata)
(Isoperla bilineata)

MEDIUM BROWNS — 3
LITTLE YELLOW
GREEN STONEFLIES — 3

THE LITTLE YELLOW STONEFLY
(Alloperla caudata)

THE LITTLE GREEN STONEFLY
(Alloperla inbecilla)

BIG GOLDENS — 2

EMERGENCE TABLE FOR WEST

WINTER-SPRING

	JANUARY	FEBRUARY	MARCH	APRIL	MAY	JUNE	JULY	AUGUST	SEPTEMBER	OCTOBER
MIDNIGHT										
8 P.M.										
4 P.M.						WESTERN SALMON-FLY (1)				
NOON				E. B. STONE (1)	(1)					
8 A.M.		TINY WINTER BLACKS								
4 A.M.										

THE TINY WINTER BLACKS
(Capnia gracilaria)
(Capnia brevicaudata)
(Nemoura cintipes)
(Nemoura oregonensis)

EARLY BROWN STONE
(Brachyptera nigripennis)
(Brackptera pacifica)

WESTERN SALMON FLY
(Pteronarcys californica)

SMALL WESTERN SALMON·FLY
(Pteronarcella badia)

SUMMER

	JANUARY	FEBRUARY	MARCH	APRIL	MAY	JUNE	JULY	AUGUST	SEPTEMBER	OCTOBER
MIDNIGHT										
8 P.M.						THE LITTLE YELLOWS				(3)
4 P.M.										
NOON						MEDIUM BROWNS		(3)		
8 A.M.						BIG GOLDENS			(2)	
4 A.M.										

WESTERN BIG GOLDENS
(Acroneuria pacifica)
(Acroneuria californica)
(Classenia sabulosa)

THE MEDIUM BROWNS
(Isoperla fulva)
(Isoperla patricia)
(Isogenus tostonus)
(Isogenus elongatus)

THE LITTLE YELLOW STONEFLY
(Alloperla pallidula)
(Alloperla signata)

THE LITTLE GREEN STONEFLY
(Alloperla delicata)

Though produced by separate groups of the species, the seasonal distribution of the stonefly demonstrates a similar chronological order of emergence in both halves of the country. Each stonefly group, either in the East-Midwest or in the West, tends to follow the other in seasonal time of appearance.

Even when we consider that the emergence cycle of each group is really the result of more than one species, there are time factors involved, with each species tending to reach maximum abundance one at a time, usually for a period of only a few days. However, their hatches cannot help but overlap. Time factors among stonefly groups, even among species *within* each group, are also evident in species of other aquatic insects, mayflies and caddisflies included. Why such a grand design of nature has resulted is best understood when we stop to consider that each species is compelled to occupy an available niche in the scheme of things. This causes direct competition to be reduced. In the confined world of the trout, such competition would be for the limited amount of food available along the bottom of the stream, of which the nymphs and larvae of each species must make quick use just prior to maturity. Often, when two closely related species must share a river system, they will "split" it between themselves. A classic case of this is the two *Pteronarcys* species that produce the salmonfly hatch in western waters. *Pteronarcys californica* and *princeps* share the same waters, but the first species is the most important to the angler because it lives in rivers located at elevations up to 7,000 feet. *Princeps* will be found most commonly in higher elevations.

Deviations of Seasonal Emergences

The effect of the *average* altitude and longitude of a given area of the country may advance or delay the overall emergence of stoneflies. For the dates cited in the eastern-midwestern timetable, we have chosen the times of the season when stoneflies hatch out of northern trout streams. These are the streams of southern New York and northern Pennsylvania, Michigan, and Wisconsin. Western emergence times are applicable to southern Montana and the uppermost parts of Wyoming, and also to Idaho and Oregon. Lower longitudinal zones in the East, such as Maryland and Virginia and west to Missouri, will experience the hatches three to four weeks sooner, and Colorado, Utah, and northern California will experience the hatches that much earlier than the times stated in the Western Emergence Table.

Local altitudinal differences, even in a specific area, have the effect of advancing or delaying a seasonal cycle. Such local deviations are most relevant to the western angler, whose rivers may vary drastically in altitude throughout their long courses. It should be remembered that any altitudinal or longitudinal differences will influence all groups by approximately the same time. The nearly predictable sequence of seasonal emergence of the stonefly groups will be basically preserved in most cases.

Climatic deviations from year to year can also have a noticeable effect on when the entire cycle will take place in a specific locale. This is evident in mountainous areas capable of holding snowpacks, where delay in melting in the spring may maintain the water at a temperature much colder than usual. This may delay the time of hatches up to three weeks.

The two factors that enable a stonefly to emerge during a specific time of the season or at a particular time of the day are water temperature and photoperiod (length of daylight). To what degree either of these factors influences the emergence of each stonefly species is apparently complex. However, enough consistencies are exhibited by the majority of the species to allow us to make certain practical generalizations.

In order for the nymphs of any species to emerge, they must reach full maturity. Growth to maturity in stoneflies occurs during times when the water temperature passes the freezing point. This enables them to emerge during winter. The tiny winter blacks begin to reach full maturity when the temperature of the water reaches 33 to 37 degrees and early black and early brown stones in the lower 40-degree range. The downstream sections of a river will almost always be first to experience emergences, and the hatching activity will slowly travel upstream. In western mountains that progression may take some time to be completed.

A drastic example of this is the common little species *Capnia gracilaria,* which first appears at 4,000 to 5,000 feet in January and will not emerge until April at 7,000 feet. Yet a closely related species, *Capnia brevicaudata,* which follows it in seasonal succession, will appear at *all* altitudes during the first three weeks of April, in waters that may differ in temperature as much as 25 degrees. Its seasonal emergence is dependent solely on photoperiod, namely those first twenty to twenty-five days of the year attaining a specific number of daylight hours. The point of this example is certainly not to give the reader the impression that he must be aware of all the biological facts governing each species in order to encounter their hatches; rather, it is to show him that wherever he chooses to fish, in any part of the country, he stands to encounter some type of stonefly, and that different waters are inhabited by different species whose dependency for seasonal emergence may be either on water temperature, photoperiod, or a combination of both. Often, when none of the hatches or adult activity is taking place in one stretch of the river, it may be doing so in either direction, upstream or down.

Time of emergence occurs in the winter-spring stoneflies at midday, with some exceptions. These early-season emergers appear to be in search of warmth, thus their hatches take place approximately between 11 A.M. and 4 P.M. The members of the summer fauna appear to be more preoccupied with escaping the hottest part of the day, and, with the exception of cool, overcast days, they will usually emerge during the evening, night, or early-morning hours. On the other hand, their adult activity, which is of concern to the angler, is not confined to such an irregular timetable.

The Life Cycle of Stoneflies

The specialization exhibited by stoneflies is the inevitable result of innumerable generations of adaptation to their environment. No better example of this exists than that of their unique life cycle. It is distinctly different from that of the mayflies or caddisflies. Nymphal life may begin shortly after the eggs are oviposited by the adult female into the stream. In the case of the summer species, nymphal life will not begin until after a long diapause (period in which development is suspended). The immediate hatching or long delay are defense mechanisms. In the winter-spring types, the diminutive nymphs leave the egg quickly (within three weeks) and burrow deep into the bottom of the stream well in advance of the often dangerously low- or warm-water conditions of summer. The nymphal forms of the summer emergers are better off surviving these adverse conditions by retaining the protection of the eggs, because of the lack of time to do otherwise.

The underside of a stonefly nymph, showing gills

While all stoneflies are herbivores in their early nymphal life, certain types become carnivores soon after attaining about a quarter of their growth. Being herbivorous or carnivorous is not a function of size; it actually depends on when the nymphs accomplish their growth for the year. Winter-spring members are the most active and grow fastest during the first five months of the year. This coincides with that period in which trout streams support liberal amounts of decaying leaves deposited the previous fall. Thus the fierce-looking *Pteronarcys* nymph is mainly a herbivore at the outset and remains so throughout its entire life. Summer emergers, which enter a long egg diapause, do not hatch until late in the year and will not attain appreciable proportions until the following spring or the beginning of summer. They then become carnivorous, feeding on the abundant aquatic life (mayfly nymphs and caddisfly and midge larvae) that overruns the bottom of most trout streams. The best example is the large *Acroneuria* (Big Golden) and related types. These are fierce in appearance and carnivorous in nature—a dangerous adversary that all aquatic insects must escape from or be eaten by.

The mechanics of actual emergence, which begin to take place once the desirable water temperature or photoperiod is achieved, are exemplified by the nymphs crawling to shore on the stream bottom and up on half-submerged rocks or any other suitable object at the margin of the stream. If there is one basic consistency among stoneflies, it is this aspect of their life cycle. The adults then will require ten to fifteen seconds to emerge out of the nymphal shuck. The adults must wait some moments before their

A stonefly nymph ready to start a new instar *J. Frederic Oswalt*

soft bodies and wings harden, then they will scurry away to a hiding place in the streamside vegetation or simply fly away to nearby trees. Some species of the little *Capnia* barely venture far and will spend their entire four-week adult life within close proximity of where they appeared from the stream. The larger types capable of good flight usually fly away to the trees. Semiwingless forms have no choice but to remain close by.

The same nymph
with its skin splitting
J. Frederic Oswalt

A typical
stonefly adult

Selection of rock, log, or willow as an emerging site along the margin of a stream appears to be general and arbitrary. However, some species exhibit a preference for certain places and for objects of a specific material, structure, or color. The reasons for this are not clearly understood by entomologists or amateur observers. Even a plausible explanation remains to be offered for such behavior.

Another unusual aspect of the biology of stoneflies, of general interest though of little concern to the fly fisher, is the fact that the males of an emerging species will hatch before the females. Males often exhibit short, useless wings that make it impossible to fly away from the stream. Perhaps this is another way nature insures their availability for the mating and fertilization of the eggs of the females that follow. This may increase the odds of the long-run survival of these types. Unlike mayflies and caddisflies, the ability to fly appears to be of little advantage to stoneflies. Wide dispersal of stonefly adults, either male or female, is positively discouraged by natural circumstances. After the mating process takes place, the females need only enough flight capability to oviposit their eggs in the riffles or margins of the stream.

Mating in most species takes place among the rocks, logs, or vegetation bordering a stream or river, usually during the day in plain view of the streamside observer. The courtship is preceded by the "drumming" of the males, reminiscent of the behavior exhibited by species of grouse. This drumming is accomplished by the males striking their abdomens on the ground or on the object on which they are resting. The females will respond to the specific beat made by the males of its species. The frequency of this signaling may differ among members of the same species inhabiting the same river in different places. This is perhaps the most straightforward proof of the extreme localization of the populations of stoneflies inhabiting our trout streams and the minimization of exchange even among the "tribes" of the same species in the same waters.

Actual copulation and fertilization is accomplished by the male climbing upon the back of the female, the male draping the lower half of its abdomen around the female's body, causing the genitalia of the two to meet. The sight of joined pairs along the stream is often common, especially with the larger stoneflies, and it has implications for the angler. The fact that a winter or spring member, such as the salmon fly, is already copulating means that the hatch has already been taking place for some time, for as long as two, three, and even four weeks.

Also relevant to the fly fisherman is the manner in which the females choose to oviposit their fertilized eggs in the stream. It may take a variety of forms. Most exciting, from the fishing point of view, is that form in which the females scurry (not fly) from the bank over the surface of the water to the riffles, release their eggs, and rapidly scurry back to safety on the bank. Trout appear to be well acquainted with this highly vulnerable method of egg-laying and snatch the fluttering, egg-filled females with vicious rises. Other types of stoneflies, those that fly well, will fly out to riffles that reflect sunlight and literally dive-bomb into the water to disperse their egg sacs upon contact. The force of their descent and uncontrollable speed often causes them to injure their wings and become entangled in the surface film, and they flutter violently in an attempt to become airborne or to hobble back to their point of origin.

As far as the fly fisher is concerned, no other type of aquatic insect demands more careful observation of the natural to determine the best presentation than the stonefly does. The presentation will often be in a most unorthodox fashion. It should always be dictated by the naturals themselves. It may be hard to conceive that for a successful presentation one should deliberately splash an artificial on the surface of the water to mimic the landing of a large female stonefly, then strip it back, causing it to skip over the surface of the water. The important point here is that all aquatic insects are different, and it is to the advantage of the angler to use his artificial so that it has the same movement the naturals exhibit.

We conclude our discussion of the life cycle of stoneflies with the subject of their need to colonize running-water habitats permanently, to compensate for natural and accidental drift. Since the stoneflies have a long nymphal phase, one to three years, they will emerge downstream from the point at which they began their life. This is especially true of stoneflies that lead exposed lives (meaning they are not burrowers), and at such times when they are accidently dislodged during high-water periods. Natural drift also occurs as a design of nature, for the purpose of redistributing the population of a certain species. This usually takes place during the first few hours of the night, at the same time big browns feed most actively.

If the age-long colonization of moving-water habitats is to be preserved by stoneflies (and mayflies and caddisflies) they must compensate for drift at one point or another in their life cycles. Stoneflies, in particular, will compensate for drift in one of three ways. First, while still in the stream in the nymphal stage they will crawl upstream as far as three or four miles in great concentrations (summer *Acronueria*, or big goldens, cover such distances). Second, the adults will undertake land migrations just before they mate and deposit their eggs. Third, just prior to ovipositing the females will fly upstream a few miles (this is the case with stoneflies capable of good flight and most types of mayflies and caddisflies). Regardless of the way the flies compensate for drift, this points out the determination of these insects to maintain their place in the environment they share with trout and other fishes. Thus, they preserve their importance to the fly fisher as well.

In the chapters that follow we will be more specific about the stoneflies that constitute the winter-spring and summer types, and more importantly, we will concentrate on how to fish their imitations during the hatch and nonhatch periods. Now we will leave the subjects of biology, behavior, and life cycle to deal with angling approaches that will help the reader catch more fish.

A powerful four-pound Colorado River brown trout that fell for a *Pteronarcys* nymph imitation during the annual salmon-fly activity.

CHAPTER TWO

The Winter Stoneflies

IT MAY COME AS A SURPRISE TO MOST ANGLERS THAT STONEFLIES ACTUALLY ACHIEVE their greatest abundance in many trout streams during the coldest time of the year, January, February, and March. Little is known of their winter activity, and with good reason, for these stoneflies will not become evident in most streams until just before the arrival of winter, only to disappear, for the most part, by early spring. They constitute virtually the only aquatic insects to be found emerging during the first three months of the year. At these times, most fly fishermen are preoccupied with preparing their equipment for the coming season, and the harsh weather tends to discourage even the hardiest anglers from venturing out to the stream.

The earliest stonefly forms are tiny; in fact, they are the smallest stoneflies to appear for the year. The most appropriate common name for them that we can think of, when considering their proportions and coloration, is the tiny winter blacks. They are exceedingly abundant only in small to medium-size, rapidly flowing streams, from January through March, though some of their species continue to appear in such waters until early May. Late winter, however, causes the equally intensive though short-lived emergences of the more important types, the early black stones. These are limited to the East and Midwest. Unlike their seasonal predecessors, they can be found hatching profusely in the slow-flowing spring creeks as well as fast-moving freestone rivers during the first two weeks of March. They are then quickly replaced by hatches of the slightly smaller and paler, early brown stones, whose geographical range, habitat, and abundance closely resemble the smaller tiny winter blacks.

The Tiny Winter Blacks (families Capniidae, Nemouridae, and Leuctridae)

The midday emergences of these small stoneflies are a common sight in freestone rivers and streams still under the siege of winter, often while there is still ice-capping along their banks. The little nymphs and adults

Tiny Winter Black:
January–March, morning–midday

Early Brown Stone:
March–April, midday

overrun the snow banks, which may have caused some anglers to refer to them as "snow flies." For the fly fisher unable to contain himself until late winter or early spring, the tiny winter blacks (and often the early black and early brown stones) provide the only activity of any significance during these winter months. Their emergence takes place well in advance of the first traditional hatches of mayflies and caddisflies, which begin fully two months later.

STREAMSIDE IDENTIFICATION

The nymphs of the three types, or families, that make up the smallest and darkest of the stoneflies are easily recognized at streamside. Members of the Capniidae complex, which are surely the most common in trout streams, are approximately 6 mm in length and have teardrop wing pads that lie parallel to their bodies. They range in color from black to dark reddish-brown. Almost identical to them are members of the families Nemouridae and Leuctridae. *Nemoura* fall second in importance and are distinguished from *Capnia* by the general configuration of their wing pads, which lie at an angle to their bodies and resemble the outline of an upside-down maple seed. Their seasonal emergence is also different. They are most common from late winter until the middle of spring and serve to ex-

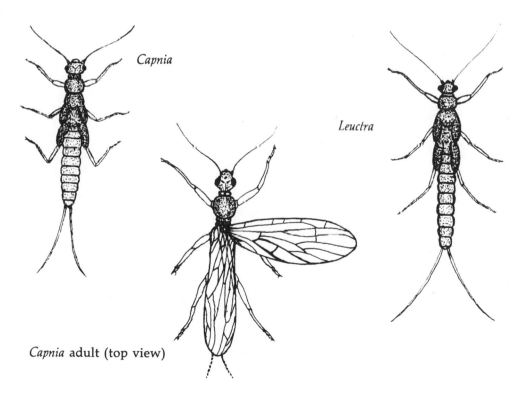

Capnia

Leuctra

Capnia adult (top view)

tend the hatches of tiny winter blacks into the legal trout season of many states. The third member of the little dark stoneflies is the family Leuctridae. They are not as important in distribution or significance as the above two types, and their nymphal forms resemble the *Capnia*, though their shape is slimmer and more cylindrical. They are occasionally important along the rocky shorelines of cold lakes.

Adults of the above types are best differentiated from each other by seasonal distribution and from other stoneflies by their small size (6–8 mm) and dark coloration. *Capnia* and *Nemoura* resemble each other, both having wings that lie flat over the abdomen when the adult is at rest. They are, however, taxonomically separable by the fact that *Nemoura* have a little X design on the foremargin of their forewings; *Capnia* do not. *Leuctra* are easily differentiated from all stoneflies by their wings, which are rolled around the abdomen. As in the nymphal stages, the adults of all three types are so close in configuration, size, and color that they can all be imitated by the single tiny winter black nymph pattern recommended in Chapter seven.

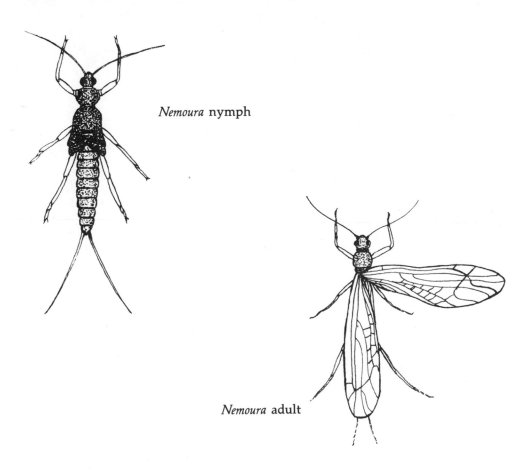

Nemoura nymph

Nemoura adult

EASTERN AND MIDWESTERN TINY WINTER BLACKS

Allocapnia granulata (family Capniidae) is the most common and abundant species in the East and can certainly serve as a representative for the other four stonefly species that help constitute the tiny winter black activity in eastern and midwestern waters. In particular, they are responsible for impressive hatches during January and February. Their importance is often complemented further by a sister species, *Allocapnia vivipara,* which in all respects resembles *A. granulata* closely. The only difference is *A. vivipara walks,* not flies, to the water where it swims underwater or scurries on the surface toward riffles to oviposit its eggs. We have often witnessed trout snatching winter stonefly adults rather deliberately, which is unlike their customarily soft rises to the adults of the tiny winter blacks, and in each case we found the deviation from custom to be the result of *A. vivipara.*

Paracapnia angulata is similarly important during April only in the East, and its significance as a hatch, if not preempted by the larger early brown stones that also emerge at this time of year, is comparable to that of *Allocapnia granulata.* Other species that continue the action of the tiny winter blacks are *Nemoura aldipennis,* the most common of the eastern stoneflies of that genus, and *Nemoura completa,* a late-April and May emerger. These insects are equally significant in the medium-size, rapid-flowing streams of the Pocono, Catskill, Adirondack, and Green mountains.

WESTERN TINY WINTER BLACKS

The great majority of western emergences of these little stoneflies is brought about by the midday hatches of *Capnia gracilaria* that are found in abundance in creeks, streams, and even large rivers, especially those with rocky bottoms. In western waters they appear at elevations of 4,000 feet as early as January and last until March. They do not reach altitudes of 7,000 to 8,000 feet until late April or May. Customarily their hatches will take place when the water temperature reaches the 40-degree mark.

Capnia in western waters are as important hatch producers as their eastern counterparts, and they can be found emerging profusely in many of the Sierra rivers, such as the Kern, the Walker River system, and many of the medium-size tributaries of Mono Creek during late winter and early spring. Small to large rivers, such as the Roaring Fork and the Frying Pan in Colorado, support their populations, as do the waters of Idaho and Montana. Even such gargantuan rivers as the Yellowstone, from the national park boundary down to its junction with the Mussleshell, have excellent and fishable hatches that take place well before the spring runoff begins.

A second species of this group that is of principal importance is *Capnia brevicaudata;* it is abundant during the first three weeks of April but its hatching lasts only a short time. Interestingly, it appears at all elevations simultaneously, demonstrating its need to emerge for the season on those first days of a specific length of daylight. The angler, however, has little need to make any species distinction among *Capnia* in western waters, for they resemble each other closely. The same holds true of western *Nemoura*. *N. cintipes,* the most common and abundant, begins to hatch at very low-altitude stretches of rivers in March and does not complete its seasonal occurrences until May. *N. besametsa* follows this emergence by approximately one month, hatching through the month of June. Both are most abundant in small or medium-size, rocky streams.

FISHING THE TINY WINTER BLACKS

The tiny winter blacks, it should be remembered, are of principal importance in freestone streams and rivers of varied size and of a microhabitat composed of large boulders to fine gravel. Perhaps the most straightforward and dependable indication of their activity and possible angling importance is the accumulation of discarded nymphal shucks on the rocks along the banks of a stream or the thick concentrations of their little adults on streamside vegetation. Their manner of emergence follows that of most stoneflies, with the nymphs migrating toward the shallows a few days prior to the actual emergence. The minute size of these nymphs makes them an insignificant morsel if they need to be chased about and fed upon singly by trout. However, their manner of accumulating in great numbers prior to the actual emergence and again when the adults complete the mating-ovipositing phase permits trout to consume them with more realistic economy. The number of nymphs that a single trout can consume of an emerging species is often surprising. It is plain to see the extent to which the little *Capnia* must accumulate in the rocky shallows of the streams they inhabit, because as many as 600 to 800 of them may fall victim to a single good-size trout during one feeding session.

To take full advantage of the opportunity offered by the hatches of these little stoneflies, trout tend to hug the banks of the stream as close as water depth will permit in order to intercept the nymphs when they crawl about and become active just before their midday emergence. The naturals are helpless little creatures when accidentally dislodged and caught in the current. They then float placidly until obtaining a solid hold on a rock or boulder or until taken by a trout. For a successful streamside approach, we recommend that the angler fish the tiny winter black nymph imitation by positioning himself approximately twenty feet from the bank (so he doesn't drive bank feeders away) and making his casts toward the bank.

Because the current near the shore usually flows more slowly than that in the middle of the stream, casts should be made with plenty of slack, us-

Duck-quill wing, small black

This pattern, with
varied coloring, serves
well for the little black
or yellow or green.

ing long, fine tippets, to achieve a dead-drift presentation that closely duplicates the free travel of the dislodged natural. The angler should three-
quarter his casts upstream, employ a constant upstream mending of the
line, and allow plenty of slack. We have found this presentation will prevent drag. With so much loose line, the angler may not perceive every

strike, but that is a small price to pay to prevent his pattern from being dragged about, warning the trout that what is coming toward it is suspect and perhaps not safe to eat.

A second fishing approach, which is necessary in waters too rapid or too deep to wade, is to fish from the bank itself. The same principles of dead-drift presentation are applicable. Now, however, it becomes a game of more exacting delivery in close quarters. The angler will have to cast his line over a rising or visible trout when fishing upstream, but he should only do so using three or four feet of tippet, preferably 5X or 6X. When fishing downstream, casts can be made up to eight feet ahead of a stationary trout and made to drift by paying out line before the artificial is within its range. The fisherman should always remember to keep his profile low when fishing downstream so he doesn't disturb the fish, which is in shallow, clear water in this situation.

The adults of the tiny winter blacks deposit their fertilized eggs at midday, specifically in riffles reflecting direct sunlight. The little females oviposit their eggs by descending hard onto the surface of the water, which inadvertantly damages their wings, and they become trapped in the surface film. Their helpless numbers will then slowly accumulate along the natural drift lanes and side eddies of the stream, and trout will begin taking as many as five or six with a single rise, developing a rhythm to their rises. Presentation should be the same as that required when fishing a fall of mayfly spinners. The timing, drift, and placement of the imitation is as much a part of the success as the imitative qualities of the artificial. The drag-free drift is the trick that causes the trout to take the artificial as confidently as it would a free-floating natural.

Early Black Stones and Early Brown Stones (family Taeniopterygidae)

In numbers, these two types of stoneflies often equal the little types we just discussed, but because of their even greater size they are much more important to the trout and the angler than their seasonal predecessors. As with the tiny winter blacks, they are midday emergers and appear during late winter and early spring. The early black stones and the early brown stones are both significant to the eastern and midwestern angler, but only the early brown stones produce good hatches in western waters.

STREAMSIDE IDENTIFICATION

At first glance the nymphal versions of these two stoneflies resemble closely that of *Nemoura.* At one time all three types were classified by entomologists under the same family. But *Taeniopteryx* (early black stones) and *Brachyptera* (early brown stones) do exhibit differences from *Nemoura* in physical aspects as well as in their biology. *Taeniopteryx* are common in varied types of eastern waters and range in average size from 12 to 14mm long, with many of the species having a distinctive white stripe along their entire length. More taxonomically exacting, they have conspicuous, retractable, little white gills at the base of each of their legs that are only evident when viewed from the underside. *Brachyptera* are usually smaller (9–11mm long), do not exhibit a stripe, and lack gills of any kind.

The adult forms have flat wings; the two are separable by their size and the fact that the adults of *Taeniopteryx* have a white spot on each base of their legs (a carry-over scar from the nymphal gills). Both of these stoneflies are found in streams only during March and April, the latest being May in the colder altitudes of the western mountain ranges.

EASTERN AND MIDWESTERN EARLY BLACK STONES AND EARLY BROWN STONES

Of all the stoneflies that emerge during the season in waters east of the Mississippi, *Taeniopteryx nivalis* (early black stone) will probably be the most abundant for no other reason than that it is a highly versatile stonefly, equally at home in slow-moving spring creeks and fast, freestone rivers. One qualification, however, must be made concerning its general importance; this species requires liberal amounts of decaying leaves along the bottom of a stream to exist. Thus, *Taeniopteryx* are usually indigenous to rivers that are bordered by hardwoods that deposit their leaves directly into the stream during the fall months. Trout rivers such as the Beaverkill in New York and the Rogue in Michigan are filled with their populations. If nature were to switch their hatches to a later slot in the year, they would probably be considered one of the top five hatches of the season. Perhaps, with the advent of no-kill regulations in more waters, carrying with them more liberal seasons, and the rising willingness of anglers to tackle the rigors of early-spring fishing, this stonefly will rise in importance. It appears at midday from late February to mid-March, and the nymphs invade the banks so actively and in such numbers it appears as if they were trying to conquer them with physical force.

By comparison, *Brachyptera fasciata,* the early brown stones, are the least common of the types we have discussed so far, but overall they turn out to be the most important. The apparent paradox of that statement is eliminated when we consider that this fly's midday hatches follow in the wake of those of the early black stones, which places them in the first weeks of the legal trout season of many states. It is the first hatch of the season in

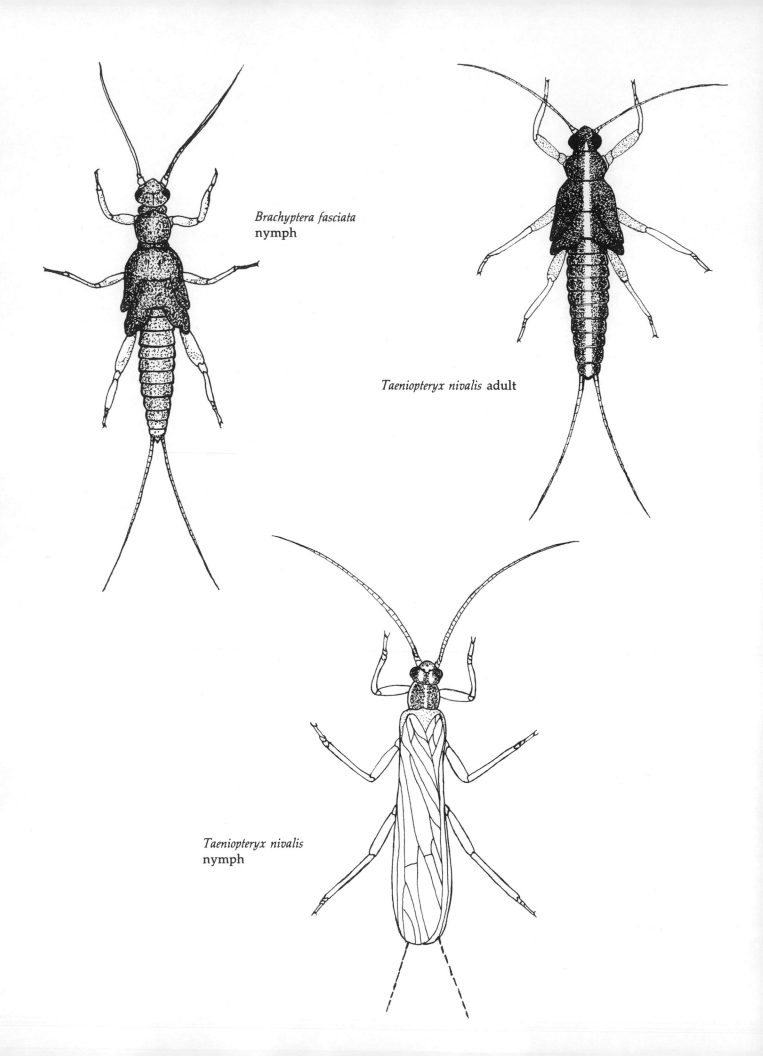

Brachyptera fasciata
nymph

Taeniopteryx nivalis adult

Taeniopteryx nivalis
nymph

New York that offers the opportunity for dry-fly fishing. This hatch often lasts until Opening Day in Michigan, Pennsylvania, and in many waters of Wisconsin.

The following information is something we feel should be pointed out to eliminate further confusion. Past angling texts state that early brown stone hatches are produced by a stonefly species named *Taeniopteryx fasciata.* It is actually *Brachyptera fasciata.* Preston Jennings first described the species in *A Book of Trout Flies* (1935), and gave it the erroneous designation. The mistake has been carried forward ever since. Regardless of their scientific nomenclature, the early brown stones are a significant hatch in most eastern trout streams during the last week of March and the first two weeks in April.

WESTERN EARLY BROWN STONES

The western early brown stones are, like their eastern counterparts, important to those anglers who fish early in the year. *Brachyptera nigripennis* is undoubtedly the most widespread, with its geographical range extending from the northern Rockies south into New Mexico and even into Arizona. We have encountered good emergences in lovely Oak Creek, just south of Flagstaff, Arizona. In the Pacific states its population is supplanted by its sister species, *Brachyptera pacifica,* most abundant in Washington, Oregon, northern California, and east into Idaho and Montana. Its range touches American trout waters again in the northern New England states, where it can be found emerging sporadically during May. The single species of *Taeniopteryx* found in western waters, *T. miopa,* is of little consequence to the western fly fisher. In many respects, the appearance of the early brown stones, in all sections of the country, signals the time to pay attention to the fishing season and to look for predictable and dependable hatches, not only of stoneflies but of mayflies and caddisflies also.

FISHING THE EARLY BLACK STONES AND THE EARLY BROWN STONES

The best indicators that a stream or river is undergoing the emergence of either of these two stoneflies are the time of year and the water temperature. March produces the best emergences (lasting well into April in western waters). More specifically, the early black stones and the early brown stones will appear when the temperature of the water ranges from 40 to 44 degrees and 44 to 48 degrees respectively. Their nymphal migrations toward the shallows prior to emergence must be a fantastic sight viewed from underwater. Trout we have caught in open water and slick runs between boulders well away from the banks have had stomachs stuffed like sausages with these nymphs. This is particularly the case during the activity of the early black stones, the imitation for which is given later and has proved deadly for us when fished dead-drift through the holding places in a stream, not just along the banks, in late winter. The same approach should be applied when fishing during the early brown stone activity later in the season.

The margins of the stream usually hold the greatest concentrations of the naturals and should never be by-passed since they are the most important locations for trout to gather to consume as many nymphs as possible with the least effort. The stream position and techniques of casting are the same as those described under the tiny winter blacks.

The female adults of the early black stones are quite large and conspicuous when they begin to deposit their eggs in the riffle sections of a river. The action then becomes a no-nonsence affair. They appear as if from nowhere, late in the afternoon, usually from high among the trees. They travel upstream a distance to compensate for natural and accidental drift, and then begin to dive-bomb into the riffles to disperse their eggs upon contact, with little regard to their well-being once they accomplish their objective. This may cause their wings to become damaged, for no sooner do they land on the water then they begin to scurry over the surface toward the safety of the banks. Their rough landing must advertise their presence to the trout, for the fish overtake them with savage rises, giving the insects little time to make it to shore.

It may sound a bit unorthodox at first, but on the fortunate occasions when we have found heavy hatches, we have done much better by landing our imitations hard on the surface of the water just above the rise, quickly mending the line to cause it to float drag free for only a foot and then retrieving it with quick strips toward the bank. The problem was not to get trout to take our artificials, but to stop them from snapping our leaders, even when we raised our tippets to the 3X and 4X sizes.

Often, when the weather is bitterly cold, the females simply land on the water and make no effort to become airborne again. We have found that a simple drag-free float over a specific trout, marked by its rising, is most effective under such conditions. Especially with this stonefly, proper presentation must always be taken into consideration. The angler is duplicating the behavior of the natural. However, no rigid rules should prevent the angler from experimenting with techniques he feels may help him to be more successful.

In all respects, the dry-fly action, or adult activity, of the early brown stones resembles that of their larger seasonal predecessors, with the exception of the female adults, which discharge their eggs while tranquilly riding the current and drift long distances before attempting flight. They are usually taken softly by trout. Their whole activity lacks the excitement of *Taeniopteryx nivalis;* however, we consider this species, because of its size and later seasonal emergence, a welcome introduction to the hatches of mayflies and caddisflies.

CHAPTER THREE

The Spring Stoneflies, or the Salmon Flies

WE HAD SEEN SEVERAL OF THE BIG RAINBOWS SLASHING AT THE LARGER FLIES AS THE flies drifted helplessly past in the fast current. Mike Lawson waded out toward one of them. Just as we looked down to admire for the last time the seven-pound rainbow one of us had caught and was releasing, we heard Mike cry out. We all looked up in time to see a great silver fish in the air. Again and again the big rainbow jumped. It crisscrossed a long stretch of the water for a full twenty minutes before giving up its exhausting efforts to regain freedom.

"I can't believe it; we've released four fish over seven pounds in a single day!" Mike cried out excitedly as he waded toward us after releasing the huge rainbow well downstream from where he first hooked him. Like children, we sat down on the bank and recalled again the different episodes of that magnificent, crisp day in mid-June on the Box Canyon stretch of the Henrys Fork of the Snake. The hatch? None other than the salmon fly, the huge black *Pteronarcys.*

The salmon flies need no introduction to most fly fishers; they are the best known of all the hatches in western waters, where their importance as big-fish producers is unique and legendary. When this hatch takes place, which can be any time between late spring and early summer, the seasonal hatches of other insects are just getting underway. As the salmon-fly nymphs invade the banks of western rivers, and their huge adults are helicoptering over the water, all other insect activities must wait their turn since they are easily overshadowed by these gargantuan stoneflies.

Three qualifications must be made concerning this impressive hatch of the largest flies found in North American waters. First, they are of principal importance in western waters and are of only local consequence in the East. (Big goldens, covered in the next chapter, are of greater importance in eastern trout streams.) Second, many of their hatches coincide with the first seasonal emergences of the big goldens, even in western waters, and with a second and smaller Pteronarcidae type, *Pteronarcella.* The big goldens and the *Pteronarcellas* often emerge with the *Pteronarcys* and augment their effect on trout. Third, the salmon-fly hatches are brief and hard to pinpoint, though they are quite dependable. They are certainly worth searching out and remain an event that all fly fishermen should treat themselves to.

Pteronarcys and *Pteronarcella,* which together constitute the salmon-fly family Pteronarcidae, are the last members of our winter-spring complex of stoneflies to emerge for the season. Like their seasonal predecessors, their greatest importance is during the day. On the other hand, the summer stoneflies, which are covered in the following chapter, become most active and hatch at dusk, night, or early in the morning; they are specifically important in distant stages, the big goldens as nymphs and the medium browns and little yellows and greens as egg-laying adults. But the salmon fly is important in all stages and under many circumstances.

Mike Lawson with a big rainbow he took from the Box Canyon of the Henrys Fork on a salmon fly

Pteronarcys californica adult

The Salmon Flies (Genus Pteronarcys)

Of both genera described in this chapter, *Pteronarcys* are the most important to fly-fishing. They are the ones that provide the impressive salmon-fly hatches in western waters and to a lesser extent in eastern waters between late spring and early summer.

STREAMSIDE IDENTIFICATION

The *Pteronarcys* forms are instantly recognized by their large size, general configuration, and dark coloration, making them almost unmistakable when encountered in the stream. They exhibit a stiff-looking pointed plate as a prothorax and a double set of wing pads whose apexes point away from the body. In color, they range from black to reddish-brown and usually have two faint stripes running the length of each side of the abdomen. Their gills are a further giveaway in that they are conspicuous and because they are present in the first two segments of the abdomen. The easiest way to identify the adults is by their size (32 to 40mm) and the obvious network of crossveins throughout the entire area of the forewing. Furthermore, they always have dark orange thoraxes, which serve to distinguish them from the often equally large adults of the big goldens, which exhibit yellowish thoraxes.

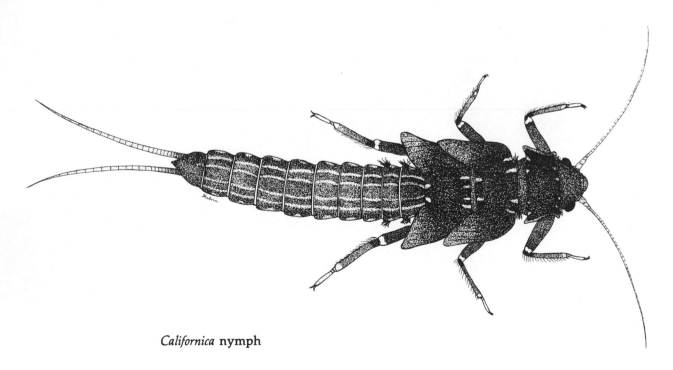

Californica nymph

EASTERN AND MIDWESTERN SALMON FLIES

The salmon flies are most often associated with western waters, where they produce an extremely important and exciting hatch. Their eastern counterparts, on the other hand, are secondary in importance to a great number of hatches of mayflies and caddisflies that occur during the early season. Nonetheless, when considering their importance at a local level, they can cause excellent fishing. *P. dorsata* is the most common species of this genus in the East and Midwest. They are most abundant in cool, clear-running streams and rivers that offer any type of riffle stretches. They may also be found in rather quiet streams.

Most hatches that we have observed took place from late April to early June. The greatest majority of these flies hatch during early evening. In the middle of May, however, they can be found hatching during warm mornings. Though they lack the concentration and numbers of their counterparts in the West, a nymphal imitation will often hook some large fish during their emergence or spinner flight. We have encountered fine hatches on the Rogue and Pere Marquette rivers in Michigan. Many of the medium-fast streams of Pennsylvania's Cumberland and Pocono areas, as well as those in the more mountainous parts of New York and the New England states, have good populations. Of late, we have also received many reports of their presence in and have collected species from the Atlantic-salmon rivers of the East, as far north as Ungava Bay in Canada.

For some time, our good friend Mike Kimball has tried to entice us to fish the brief but exciting emergence in the lovely Delaware River, which runs between New York and Pennsylvania in its upper reaches, and de-

Jorgensen's big black
stonefly nymph

spite our efforts to meet this hatch on this river, we have not yet been successful. We asked Mike to give us his impression of the river itself, and we found his reply so interesting and representative of eastern fishing during the *P. dorsata* hatch that we opted to quote him. Here's what he had to say:

"Both as an insect factory and as a natural hatchery for large rainbow trout, the Delaware River rivals the prestigious Henrys Fork of the Snake. I know of no other place in the East where a population of large rainbows has a choice of such a wide variety of insect life as they do in the Delaware. Even by western standards, the river is large. Originating from mountain runoff and each flowing through a dam, at the Pepacton or Cannonsville reservoirs, the East and West branches join forces at Hancock, New York, and begin a journey through the Catskill Mountains; in places it's as remote as almost any eastern wilderness water.

"Knowledgeable Delaware fishermen look forward each June to the appearance of a brief but productive stonefly hatch, the center of attraction of which is the *Pteronarcys dorsata.* In terms of sheer numbers, the Delaware's stoneflies cannot compare to the legendary hatches of such Montana notables as the Madison and Big Hole rivers. But, like its western counterparts, it enjoys a daylight emergence of large stoneflies, a not-so-common event in eastern waters. The *P. dorsata* hatch can begin as early as three or four P.M. and can continue well past the closing time of nearby Hancock's 'watering holes.'

"Harry Darbee in his popular book, *Catskill Flytier,* talks about important Delaware River stonefly hatches during the glory years of the Catskills. In those years, they appeared by sunrise on mornings of early June, shortly after the appearance of the Green Drakes *(Ephemera guttulata).* More recently, I have found the *P. dorsata* hatch to coincide with heavy Pale Evening Dun *(Ephemerella dorothea),* emergences again shortly after the first appearances of the Green Drakes, but not as an eye-opening dawn hatch but as an afternoon and early-evening hatch. Emergence times may have changed from the Theodore Gordon era, but the preference shown by fish above eighteen inches for this hatch remains as strong as ever.

"The coexistence of these stoneflies with heavy sulphur-mayfly activity can result in a 'masking-hatch' situation, with a slight variation. Whereas a masking hatch commonly conceals a fish's preference for a small fly over a more obvious (and often more numerous) larger fly, exactly the reverse is the case in the Delaware, since the abundance of the comparatively small sulphurs can camouflage the large rainbow's preference for the bulky but scarcer stoneflies.

"It does appear that it is the food value not the numbers that is of interest to these rainbows. I have frequently witnessed a similar situation while fishing some of the Adirondack's well-known freestone rivers, where often the good fish ignore a heavy late-season *Isonychia* spinner fall in preference to an autumn brood of *P. dorsata.* So, likewise, the trophy fish of the Delaware prefer the bulk of a stonefly to the relatively plentiful, but diminutive sulphurs. This premise seems to hold true whenever stoneflies appear in reasonable numbers, thus violating the 'multiple-hatch' axiom that says fish always prefer the most prevalent insects on the water.

"I have watched the best fish of the Delaware near Lordsville, New York, literally stack up at the tails of its football-field-like pools waiting for the adult stoneflies. The first signs of insect movement can send these rainbows many feet from their feeding stations to reach a struggling adult. The eagerness with which these fish thrash around for the early-evening meal is the giveaway to the puzzle of this masking-hatch situation. There is little telltale surface disturbance when the *Ephemerella* spinners are being sipped; but when the elusive stonefly is captured, the attacking trout will often displace the equivalent of its weight in splashing water. The enthusiasm of these rainbows can lead the novice fisherman into delusions of easy pickings, but nothing could be further from the truth. It would be difficult to find any more selective stonefly fishing than on the super-slick eddies of the Delaware River.

"The size and 'dance' of the stonefly protect the fish from the fisherman. The answer to fooling these fish is in understanding how to dance a stonefly. Just as too much action given to a stonefly imitation can send a good fish rocketing for cover, so can the gentlest twitch delivered in the wrong place put that same fish down. The real secret becomes *where* to impart the action to the fly. It should be outside of its window of vision that this induced fluttering action occurs. Outside the perimeter of the fish's cone of vision, the fish appears less able to detect the imperfect action imparted to a large fly. It is outside these visual boundaries that skittering an imitation of a stonefly becomes a deadly technique. For it is here that the fish can't clearly detect the fraud.

"Action given to a large fly *within* the window will frequently send a sophisticated trout to its winter quarters. I suspect that any action an angler gives to a fly, and particularly to a large fly, is more or less imperfect. Thus, from a fish's point of view, when a large fly moves unnaturally within its area of visual acuity, an already questionable fly becomes highly suspect. This same fly twitched outside the window, on the other hand, becomes suggestive of the natural and is consequently not subject to the same degree of scrutiny as an imitation moved within a fish's window.

"The obvious conclusion is not to cast to the traditional point two or three feet above a rise, but rather to a target considerably above the riseform. When you are fairly certain that the fly is not within the fish's range of sharp vision, impart a subtle twitch to the fly, then feed line for a drag-free float over the suspected location of the fish. This technique need not be restricted only to stonefly fishing, but can be applied to any fishing that requires large flies to which the angler imparts action. I have found it particularly effective for imitating the large caddisflies of California's Hat Creek, for suggesting the dying struggle of the Delaware's huge coffin-fly spinners, and for tempting the sophisticated rainbows along the 'grasshopper banks' of the Henrys Fork."

We have found the pattern for the important western *P. californica* (mentioned later in Chapter Seven) to more than suffice as an imitation for all three species of *Pteronarcys,* and we recommend it for the eastern *P. dorsata.* We feel that the pattern is superior to any of those we have experimented with over the years.

WESTERN SALMON FLIES

Of the fifty-six western rivers we chose for our research, nymphs of *Pteronarcys* appeared in forty-six of them. The size and tempo of these waters seemed to make little difference to the populations. We found them equally abundant in small creeks and large rivers that provided good amounts of decaying leaves, detritus, or algae as natural food for the large herbivorous nymphal forms. *P. californica* is unquestionably the dominant *Pteronarcys* in the West and proved to make up the great majority of the salmon-fly hatches. Two other species, however, were also evident and under certain circumstances could supplant the *P. californica* in population and importance. These other two species are *P. princeps* and *P. dorsata.* The first is most important in the waters of the Pacific Northwest and in the Sierras, occurring with its best hatches in the higher elevations. According to Brad Jackson, who helped us significantly in our western research, in waters near his fly shop in Redding, California, *P. princeps* constitutes a good hatch during the first two weeks of June in the McCloud River. *P. dorsata,* the same species found in eastern waters, is also found in the more northerly latitudes of the western United States.

In the West, the geographical range of *Pteronarcys* extends from the uppermost areas of the western provinces of Canada south to California, Arizona, and New Mexico. Their seasonal emergence in rivers within this extensive region is dependent upon water temperature, which differs in specific river systems as the season progresses. Thus, the salmon-fly hatch will appear first in the waters of the lower states, whose rivers first attain the optimal water temperature of 50 to 60 degrees. Rivers such as the Kings River in California will experience the hatch as early as the first week in April, while it will not appear in the slightly colder Pit River until April 20. Hat Creek has a May 15 to June 5 emergence, as do many tributaries of the Sacramento. The Yuba, Feather, and the Mokolumme have fair hatches at the same time as Hat Creek.

More northerly rivers along the Pacific Coast will undergo the salmon-fly hatches even later in the season. The Upper Deschutes hatches occur from the latter part of May until June 20, slightly earlier than the hatch occurs in the inland waterways of the tri-state area of Montana, Idaho, and Wyoming. The Henrys Fork near Ashton, Idaho, has a constant water temperature and a June 1 to June 10 timetable, though upstream in the Box Canyon area of the same river, the best occurrences are between June 10 and June 20. These are the same times as on the nearby Fall River, also in Idaho.

Yellowstone Park waters, directly warmed by geothermal processes, see the hatch from June 10 to June 25, with the exception of the much colder Yellowstone River, where the hatch is an early-July event. The hatch moves from the Gardiner River into the park between June 28 and July 20. The salmon-fly hatches take place in southwestern Montana waters, such as the Big Hole, Clarks Fork and the Blackfoot, during the latter half of June (June 18 to June 30) while the colder Madison begins to see hatches on June 25. Then the hatch crawls upstream four or five miles a day until it reaches the Quake Lake area by July 15. Colorado rivers have dependable hatches during the first three weeks of June; on the Gunnison, Roaring Fork, and the Frying Pan the hatches customarily take place between June 1 and June 22.

Bear in mind that determining the exact date of a salmon-fly hatch in a specific river is almost as difficult as predicting a game of roulette. Moreover, rivers influenced by cold springs throughout their lengths, will have the hatch repeatedly delayed at the confluence of these springs. Stretches of water protected from the warming rays of the sun, by high-walled canyons for example, will have a similar delay. Nonetheless, many consistencies are demonstrated by the hatch in all waters, and, as we stated before, a temperature range of 50 to 60 degrees coincides with the better activity. The best activities are at such times when the water temperature is from 55 to 58 degrees at midday (eleven A.M. to four P.M.). Semicloudy days, as may be expected, are the best and most conducive to *Pteronarcys* nymph activity and availability to trout.

All that has been said so far may suggest that the actual hatch takes place from midday to late afternoon. It does not. The nymphs start to become active during the middle of the day along the bottom of the river, and the adults then begin to forage about and oviposit later in the day. However, the actual emergence of *Pteronarcys* nymphs occurs mostly toward the evening hours, or at night, though their actual hatching is anticlimactic and adds nothing to the great numbers in which the nymphs are available to the trout during the late-morning hours. The angler's objective is to fish when the nymphs first become active and are subject to predation by trout, before the fish become gorged with their numbers. Thus, late morning is the best time to start fishing.

Fishing one of these hatches is exciting business and it is little wonder that anglers from all over the country flock to those waters that have good populations of these large flies. The first streamside indication that a specific river is undergoing a salmon-fly hatch is provided by the large *Pteronarcys* adults that can be seen hanging on the trees, logs, and bushes that border the banks. Local information from tackle shops is often quite reliable and should be sought out. From a seasonal point of view, the best time to begin to fish with the big *Pteronarcys* imitations is at the beginning of the hatch. It is then the trout become aware of the large numbers of available naturals and begin to forage actively for them. As the hatch progresses, trout will migrate to the shallows along with the main concentration of the nymphs, transforming the fishing strategy to that of bank fishing and closer casting.

Once the hatch is at its peak, and the adults along the banks are already beginning to mate, it becomes a much tougher game, a matter of competition between the numerous naturals and the angler's single imitation. It is to the fisherman's advantage to use a nymph during the morning hours, before the trout have fully consumed their daily meal, and again toward evening when the nymphs are undergoing their actual emergence from the stream and are becoming available to the trout in the greatest numbers.

Black and big golden shucks

Noon through the afternoon hours is best for dry-fly fishing to mimic the accidental falling or deliberate descent of the adults into the water to deposit their eggs.

As the emergence wanes in a given area, it is signaled by the drifting of fresh nymphal shucks along the margins of a specific stretch of river. Customarily, about a week or two after the beginning of a hatch, an artificial nymph can be used to search the water, as hungry trout will still be looking for stray naturals. For a period of two or even three weeks after the hatch, imitations of the adults, which can still be seen flying around completing the ovipositing phase of their life cycle, can provide exciting dry-fly fishing.

Using a nymph imitation will usually outproduce any dry-fly pattern during the actual hatch. Who can argue, however, with the excitement of a large brown or rainbow snatching a big dry fly with a vicious and nerve-racking rise? Despite their large size, *Pteronarcys* nymphs are hapless creatures when caught in the main current or along the slower-moving water near the banks. Thus, the presentation of the imitation requires no more movement than a dead drift with the current. Nymph fishing before or at the beginning of the seasonal hatch should be done over all holding places in a river. The nymphs will be gathering in protected pockets before beginning their shoreward migrations. Above all, flies should be fished *deep*, so deep that the angler actually feels the imitation bumping the bottom.

The best stream position for making the cast, whether to the natural holding places in a river before the hatch has begun, or along the banks after it has started, is upstream from the target. A cast is made quartering upstream to minimize the amount of drag-producing crosscurrents the line will traverse, allowing the fly to sink to the bottom. As it nears the bottom, the angler should twitch it slightly to give it the subtle motion of a momentarily wiggling natural and again let it sink and dead drift through a holding place or an area with a rising trout. But the fisherman should always keep in mind that he should never position himself exactly upstream from a run or rising fish he expects to fish for. He should always angle himself from it so he doesn't warn the trout of his presence by dislodging material from the bottom. Fishing the banks is the most common and effective approach during most of the salmon-fly hatch and the best position is within twenty feet of the bank. Upstream casts to let the artificial sink *deep* before it reaches the target are recommended. The angler should play out plenty of line in the process if need be. The slightest hesitation in the line should always be treated as a take. Often when a fly is intercepted, the line will merely stop its travel without a noticeable commotion. We highly recommend this downstream approach to a fish.

Dry-fly fishing allows, of course, more telltale indications from the trout. They snatch these large stoneflies with unmistakable and often thrilling rises. In the absence of the adult naturals and a rise of trout in the middle of the river, dry-fly fishing should be confined to the banks, preferably just under the overhanging bushes along a river. Optimally, it should be to a specific trout that the fly fisher has noticed rising. The presentation of the artificial should simulate the action of the naturals. The most common scenario is when the adults accidently drop onto the surface of the water, flutter briefly but violently, ride the surface film calmly for ten or twenty feet, then resume their fluttering in an effort to gain the safety of the bank. The angler should drop his artificial approximately ten feet above the rise, twitching it slightly within the first five feet, which gives it the fluttering effect of a natural and advertises it to nearby trout. Then he should let it ride smoothly over the fish. Watching a few adults drift over a rising fish offers the best indication of its position and of how the presentation should be made.

PATTERNS FOR WESTERN SALMON FLIES

All that has been recommended so far would suggest that heavily weighted nymphs be used to get them to the bottom. For years we have looked for a simple-to-tie (meaning that five or six can be tied in an hour), effective pattern that is suggestive of the natural and that meets our standards. The pattern Mike Lawson was so kind to reveal to us a few seasons past is the one we consider the best and most practical that we know of for the salmon-fly hatch.

More fanciful nymph imitations work just as well in many circumstances. However, they are time consuming to tie and expensive to buy, and they are often of such stiff, prickly material that we question their overall value. It has often been our experience that trout appear able to take and release an imitation lacking the soft, pliable feel of a natural faster than a person can wink an eye. In most situations during the salmon-fly hatches in medium- to fast-running streams trout neither have the time nor the inclination to inspect the imitation closely. Mike Lawson's nymph pattern takes into consideration the best of many innovations of different fly tiers. He combines their best features into a single, easy-to-tie, and extremely effective new pattern. The curved hook style, in which this imitation should be tied, imitates closely the manner in which the nymphs of *Pteronarcys* coil when they are dislodged and drift along the bottom of the stream. It also lessens the chances of snagging the imitation when it is fished properly, bumping the bottom.

Mike has also devised a dry-fly imitation for this hatch that has the same practical and imitative virtues that his nymph pattern has. Perhaps its greatest attribute is that it is extremely effective during the times when trout become selective to the adults. It has the same low configuration of

Clipped deer-hair
salmon fly

Improved salmon fly

the natural, floats remarkably well, and withstands the punishment of landing fifteen or twenty trout. A second dry-fly pattern Mike ties for this hatch improvises on the Sofa Pillow, a favorite dry fly of western anglers for the salmon-fly hatch. Mike's version increases the Sofa Pillow's floating capabilities tremendously. It requires less false casting and dressing, which leaves more time to fish during the hatch. Both of these dry flies and the nymph pattern are fully described in Chapter Seven.

Pteronarcella nymph

Stacked deer-hair stone

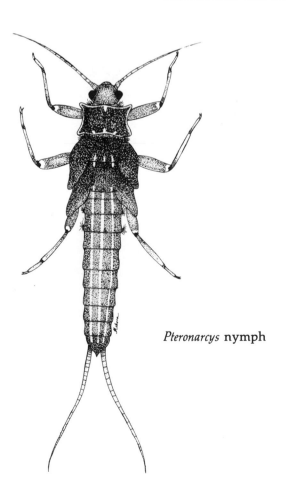

Pteronarcys nymph

The Small Western Salmon Flies (Genus Pteronarcella)

This strictly western stonefly, the *Pteronarcella,* is at first glance a small version of the type we have just discussed, and, as far as we know, the *Pteronarcella* has received no mention in angling books to date. It deserves attention from at least the western angler, since it often accompanies the hatches of the larger *Pteronarcys.* In our experience, it appeared on several occasions in such numbers during the hatch of the larger type that it caused the trout to become aware of its specific size, and they began to refuse the larger imitations of its more common sister genus.

STREAMSIDE IDENTIFICATION

These nymphs are identical to those of *Pteronarcys* except that they have gills on the first three abdominal segments, rather than only on the first two as is the case with the *Pteronarcys* nymphs. When mature, they are easily distinguished from *Pteronarcys* by size, averaging only 22 to 25mm versus the larger proportions of the *Pteronarcys* nymphs (32 to 40mm). Moreover, they usually exhibit three faint stripes instead of two (as in the case of the *Pteronarcys*), on each side of the abdomen. Adults are practically identical to the larger *Pteronarcys,* but are, of course, much smaller. Size is the most practical feature to use to tell the two apart, both being almost identical in all other respects, including the complete network of cross-veins on the forewings shown by the adult.

Our first introduction to this smaller salmon fly occurred during a salmon-fly hatch on the Madison River. We had just begun fishing and combing the margins along the willows. From the outset we received false rises from trout after trout before we became aware of the presence of the smaller *Pteronarcella* clinging to the branches of the streamside vegetation as the larger salmon flies were doing. They were much more numerous and available to the trout in this particular stretch, and a small imitation, on a #8 hook, produced better for us and resulted in more dependable rises. Upon returning to West Yellowstone and inquiring in the fly shops, we found that none carried a pattern for this stonefly. In fact, no one was aware of the fly's presence or possible importance in the local rivers.

Pteronarcella certainly don't compare in importance to the larger *Pteronarcys;* however, on many occasions we have witnessed their activity, which supplanted, temporarily at least, the importance and numbers of the big salmon fly. Rivers such as Rock Creek, the Bitterroot, and the Big Hole in southwestern Montana support their numbers and produce good emergences, as do the Madison (below Varney's Bridge) and the Yellowstone River (below Gardiner). The Roaring Fork in Colorado and the Colorado

River have good hatches, as does the slow-flowing Fall River in California. In all these cases, the particular species was either *P. badia* or *P. regularis,* and we recommend using the imitation for the big goldens described in Chapter Seven.

We do not suggest that *Pteronarcella* are a major hatch in western waters (the only part of the country in which they are found), but we simply choose to convey to the reader our personal experiences with their hatching and their significance at times. In case the angler comes upon a stretch of river where they are available to trout in good numbers, switching to the smaller imitation given for the similar-size big golden may result in a most pleasant and welcome surprise. The fly fisher should always remember that even species that are generally uncommon are often locally abundant and can be important, producing intensely selective feeding.

CHAPTER FOUR

The Summer Stoneflies

PERHAPS YOU CAN RECALL FISHING QUIETLY ON A STREAM DURING A SUMMER TWILIGHT, when suddenly hundreds of delicate yellow and green flies began descending on the water, causing pandemonium. You may already be familiar with these stonefly forms that awaken trout from the doldrums of warm water temperatures, providing excellent summer angling.

June, July, and August bring many changes in the aquatic insects in our trout streams. There are changes in coloration, size, and the time of daily emergence. Stoneflies are no exception. The summer fishing season coincides with the time that stoneflies make their most pale and colorful appearance, with many members being yellow, green, or golden. Another interesting transformation is that, as summer progresses, stoneflies become smaller. Last, unlike the midday emergers of fall and spring, summer stoneflies become most active (hatching and egg laying) during the early morning and late afternoon.

Certain points should be kept in mind when distinguishing the differences between the summer and the winter and spring stoneflies and their importance to the angler. The winter forms, such as the tiny winter blacks, emerge during the coldest part of the year. Their emergences are impressive in many medium- to fast-running streams, but they precede Opening Day in many states. The emergences of their next-larger successors, the early black and brown stones, last well into the fishing season. They are extremely important in most trout streams because they emerge early enough to receive no competition from mayflies or caddisflies. The salmon flies produce one of the best and most impressive emergences of the entire year. Unfortunately, they are not found throughout the country; generally their flush hatches are confined to western and far northern waters.

The summer stoneflies exhibit many differences from the earlier emergers. The big goldens, the first to appear in summer, are quite common, but do not produce impressive or dependable flights. This is because their emergence is difficult to encounter with any degree of consistency during the daylight hours. Most of their hatches occur at night. Nonetheless, because of their abundance and large size, they are a permanent mainstay of a trout's diet during the summer months. Perhaps no other type of aquatic insect, when imitated in its nymphal form, has successfully caught more large trout during nonhatch periods than those of the big goldens. The adults are also great for night fishing in the East.

The second most important summer stoneflies to the angler are the medium browns. They are most common during June and July in most trout streams. Unlike the big goldens, these stoneflies are most significant when the adult form is depositing fertilized eggs back into the stream. Their spinner activity usually takes place during the morning or evening hours, when they normally manage to entice trout to surface-feed. Their true emergence may be encountered at times—but this stage lacks the numbers and the dependability of the adults. Cloudy, unseasonable summer days are the exception and will cause the medium browns to produce their most concentrated and fishable emergences. The same rule holds true for the hatching and egg-laying of the little yellows and greens, which in some ways resemble the habits of the larger yellows and browns.

The smaller stoneflies belong to a different taxonomic family, and this third group of summer stoneflies is the little yellows and greens. They demonstrate more obvious and unique coloration, which ranges from dull amber to a striking bright green. Their seasonal cycle begins in late spring, but they become more important to the fly fisher from midsummer to late fall. For what they lack in size, they certainly make up for in numbers. At times they literally carpet stretches of water and cause trout to become quite selective to their diminutive size, unusual color, and their behavior. The little yellows and greens take the general seasonal cycle of stoneflies to the end of the fishing season in many waters and are the last of the stoneflies to appear for the year.

So many similarities are demonstrated by the summer stoneflies in all sections of the country that it takes no more than three different artificial patterns to imitate them all. Fishing these artificials will be covered in Chapter Five, which deals with tackle, techniques, and tactics. There is a specific approach used when fishing the nymph of the big goldens when no hatch is taking place, a profitable course to employ at all times when no emergence is evident on the stream. Chapter Five will also cover the techniques for fishing the adult imitations of the medium browns and the little yellows and greens when they fall in great numbers on the surface of the water and cause trout to devour them.

The Big Goldens (Family Perlidae)

The discarded shucks of the big golden nymphs are probably the most frequently encountered among the rocks along a trout stream. Since they require two or even three years to attain full maturity, they are always collectible in varying sizes from trout streams. Their striking markings make them easy to recognize.

STREAMSIDE IDENTIFICATION

Big goldens exhibit a mosaic network of conspicious yellow markings on a background of either black or brown. The most telltale feature that distinguishes them from other types of stoneflies we have discussed is the simple, rounded ends of their double set of wing pads. They also have conspicuous tufts of gills on all three thoracic segments, as does the

Arcynopteryx parellela

nymph of the salmon fly, but never in the first two or three abdominal segments as is the case with the latter type of stonefly. Adults carry over the shriveled remains of the nymphal gills, making streamside recognition of big golden adults a routine matter. They are conspicuous by their large size, which often approaches the proportions of the salmon fly. Their wing venation, however, differs from that of the larger salmon fly, and the prominent row of veinlets at the base of their forewings is missing. The big golden adults lack the gill remains, or scars, in the first few abdominal segments.

EASTERN BIG GOLDENS

The activity of large stoneflies in the trout waters of the East are caused by two species in particular: *Phasganophora capitata* (originally and still commonly known in fishing circles as *Perla capitata*) and *Acroneuria carolinensis*. *P. capitata* is certainly the most abundant of the two, and, in its nymphal stage, one of the most handsome of the aquatic insects. Its best populations are encountered in rocky-bottom streams of the northeastern states,

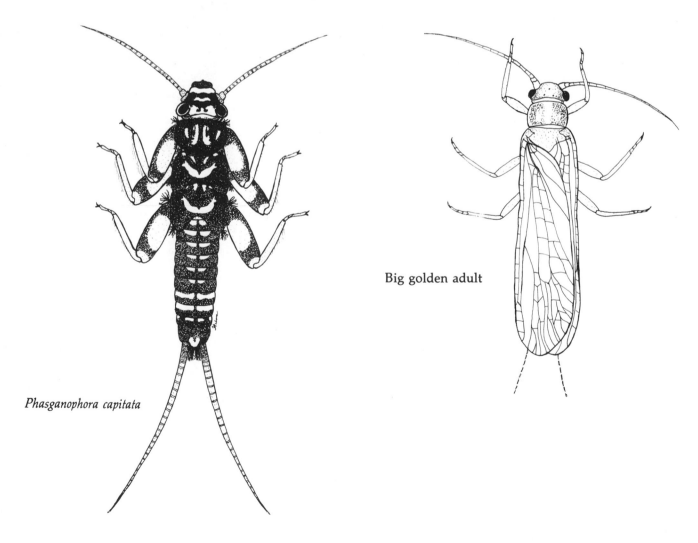

Phasganophora capitata

Big golden adult

although its range extends as far south as Georgia and Tennessee. Though some of their numbers are present in the Midwest, the placid and more silted rivers of that region are not as conducive to *P. capitata* populations as are the faster and more aerated eastern waters. The species is an early-morning emerger, with the best adult activities occurring just before nightfall, especially during June and July. Its adult activity is probably the most concentrated and reliable of all big goldens, with the large adults suddenly appearing as if from nowhere, descending onto the surface of the stream rather clumsily, and then violently fluttering about in a futile effort to become airborne again. This is a great opportunity for trout, which easily overcome the flies' frantic efforts. This is an important stonefly in both its nymphal and adult forms, and the one we choose to represent the big golden, as it is of greatest importance to the eastern angler.

A. carolinensis, the second species of the big golden group also found frequently in eastern trout streams, closely resembles *P. capitata* in general appearance and behavior. It is the species of greatest importance to those anglers accustomed to fishing small to medium-size, rapidly flowing streams and rivers. It emerges at night from midsummer to August. As with all *Acroneuria, A. carolinensis* lacks the ridge or line of minute hairs between the eyes, which is exhibited by the more common *P. capitata* nymphs, thus distinguishing these two species for the angler.

Paragentina immarginata ranks third in populations and importance. In the waters that it inhabits, and the time of year in which it becomes active, it resembles *P. capitata.* The taxonomic difference between the two is that *P. immarginata* does have the ridge of minute hairs forming a line between its eyes, but lacks the conspicuous anal gills protruding from the base of the tails.

MIDWESTERN BIG GOLDENS

Trout and salmon rivers in the Midwest are richly endowed with populations of three members of the family Perlidae. *Paragentina media* is found in excellent numbers in many of the trout waters of Wisconsin, Indiana, Ohio, and Michigan. In Michigan, rivers such as the Rogue in northern Kent County, the smooth-flowing Au Sable, and the swifter-running Pere Marquette support their numbers very well. They also inhabit the same silty stretches that support populations of burrowing mayflies, such as the *Hexagenia* mayflies. These large burrowers remain well hidden in their U-shaped houses during their nonhatch periods, and fishing the imitations of *P. media* will often outproduce that of any other aquatic insect during its seasonal cycle. Their hatches occur from the last week in June until the latter part of July, only a three-week period in any particular stretch, with the actual hatching taking place the first three hours of night. However,

Eastern big golden nymph

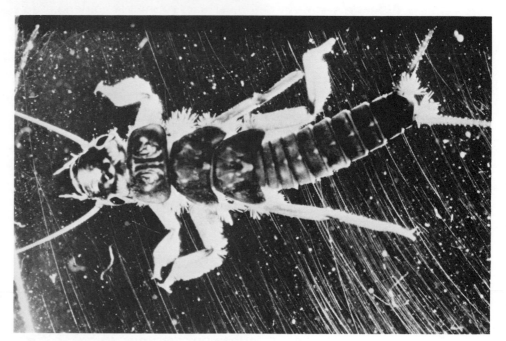

Midwestern big golden nymph

Midwestern big golden adult

we have witnessed the egg-laying activities of the adults at dusk on numerous occasions.

Acroneuria lycorias, the second stonefly found in smooth-flowing waters of the Midwest, often makes its debut two weeks before *P. media.* It demonstrates a marked tendency to emerge early in the day. This insect is important to those anglers who are on the stream as early as seven A.M. The best way to fish at that time is close to the deep banks where the large nymphs of this species congregate prior to their daily emergence. A dead-drift presentation is usually best, but the angler should watch for those occasions when the newly emerged adults accidently flop back into the water and become helpless, enticing victims for waiting trout.

The third summer stonefly of importance to the midwestern angler is *Perlesta placida.* This species stands on its own as a good hatch and a good producer for anglers at specific times of the day and year. It is a common stonefly when it makes its seasonal debut, customarily hatching between the first week of July and the middle of August. Its emergences are characterized by short, concentrated hatches that appear approximately one hour after dark, barely lasting a half hour to forty-five minutes. It is no accident that their appearance on the stream coinicides with the same time brown trout become most active. We have found that the nymph pattern given in Chapter Seven is very effective during the seasonal hatches. The adult activity begins about four to five days after their first appearance, but unfortunately when they return to the river their impact on fishing does not compare to the impact of their actual emergence.

Trout streams in the East and in the Midwest do support other stonefly populations that we have never encountered in enough numbers to merit attention. One stonefly, however, that should be mentioned is *A. ruralis,* which generally resembles the other *Acroneuria* discussed above. It lacks the conspicuous markings of its sister species, being a basically dull, colorless aquatic form. Perhaps more important is the fact that it is a hardy insect and can be found intermittently in trout waters of diverse size and composition, especially those with large amounts of debris and decaying

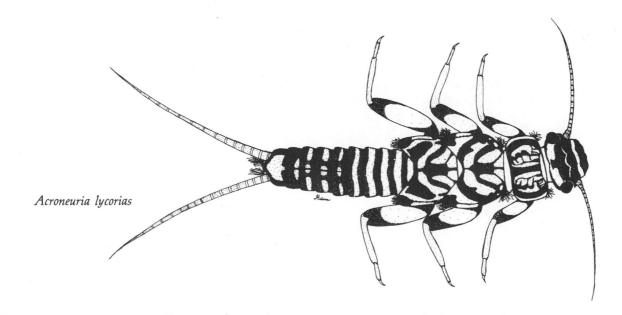

Acroneuria lycorias

leaves along their bottoms. Admittedly, many of these waters are so depleted of oxygen during the hottest months of the year that they are unable to support trout during the time *A. ruralis* emerges.

We have found the easy-to-tie pattern given in Chapter Seven a practical and effective one for the above-mentioned stonefly species. In composition it is very soft, and it effectively imitates the natural when worked through the water. It should be kept in mind that many of the waters in which big goldens are found flow quite smoothly. This gives the trout more of an opportunity to inspect an artificial or spit it out the instant it feels unnatural hardness than the trout has in faster-flowing streams.

WESTERN BIG GOLDENS

Western waters support species of big goldens in the same abundance as trout waters in the East and Midwest. Most dominant of the species is *Acroneuria pacifica,* an extremely common and early emerger during June and July. The adults usually become quite active just before nightfall. The first seasonal appearances of *A. pacifica* are usually diffused with hatches of the salmon flies and will be found in the willows along rocky-bottom, well-aerated rivers. In the Pacific states, *Acroneuria californica* will be found in equivalent numbers to those of its sister species and is well represented in the trout waters of the Sierra and the Cascade mountains. Its emergences are in July and August. Both stoneflies, *A. pacifica* and *A. californica,* are favorites with summer-run steelhead, whose stomachs are often literally crammed with the insects' large nymphs.

A third species that we have found to be as significant to the western angler as the *Acroneuria,* is the *Claassenia sabulosa,* differentiated from *Acroneuria* species by the row of minute hairs appearing as a ridge between the eyes of the nymph. It is an extremely large stonefly, emerging only after the nymphs have attained a full 32mm in length, and oftentimes approaching the proportions of the salmon fly. We have found its best populations in Rocky Mountain trout waters from Montana, Wyoming, and Idaho, south into Colorado and even New Mexico and Arizona. Its angling significance depends largely on the fact that it is a common late-season emerger, principally hatching during August and September. During this two-month period it often emerges in such numbers that rocks bordering freestone rivers are solidly covered with their discarded shucks. Though the adults become active at any time of the day (but usually between late afternoon and late morning) they do not return to the water in enough concentration to cause the same frenzied feeding by trout as the adults of the salmon flies do. Nonetheless, they do produce unusual fishing action at times, and the dry-fly pattern given later is very good for a full two months after the larger salmon flies have disappeared for the season.

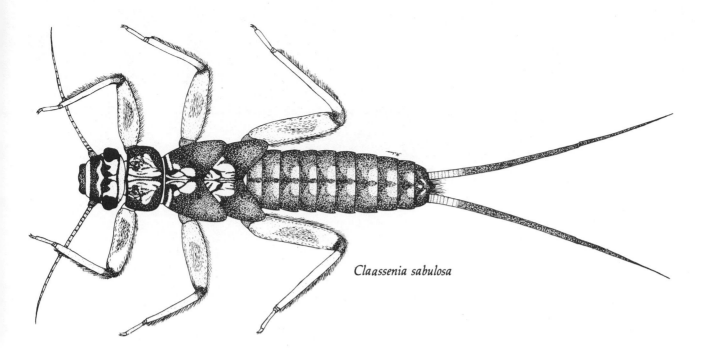

Claassenia sabulosa

While fishing late in the year on the Bitterroot River in southwestern Montana we encountered whole sections of the river's banks encrusted with the discarded shucks of *C. sabulosa* nymphs that had emerged early that morning. We had missed their emergence activity, but when we began to cast we heard explosive sounds just below us in a stretch of water lined with overhanging willows. At first it appeared as if the trout were snatching grasshoppers. We were genuinely surprised to discover that the trout were hugging the banks, then dashing out ten to twenty feet after *C. sabulosa* females that were rapidly scurrying over the surface in an effort to lay their eggs. We positioned ourselves thirty feet away, in a direct line with the willows, being careful to stay far enough away not to startle the fish. We found we could get violent takes by using the following method. We would cast ten feet upstream from a rise to avoid lining the trout, quickly mend the line upstream to reduce drag, and then, when within range of a trout, quickly twitch the imitation and strip the line to cause the artificial to skitter above the water like the natural. We had a lot of success with this method, reminiscent of late-season grasshopper fishing on Henrys Fork of the Snake. We witnessed a second such phenomenon produced by the same stonefly later in the fall while fishing the Yellowstone River in the park above Sulphur Cauldron. This time the action was with cutthroats that had lost all their summer lethargy and wariness.

Perhaps this stonefly serves as a classic example that careful streamside observation is always the best approach when fishing different types of waters with different types of emergences of aquatic insects. No number of pages in this or any other book can cover all the examples. The best we

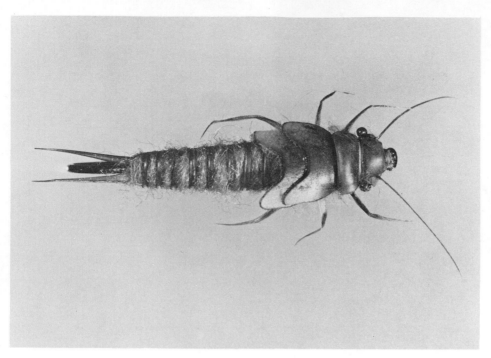

Jorgensen's big golden stonefly nymph

can do here is to give the times when you may encounter these exciting hatches and adult activities of the large and important stoneflies.

FISHING THE BIG GOLDENS

Imitations of these large stoneflies are extremely important to the angler when no activity is apparent on the water. Not only are the natural nymphs large and easily recognized by trout in their resting places at such times, but they are available to the fish twenty-four hours a day. Trout will rarely shun one of these large nymphs when it is presented correctly. When they do shun them, it is usually because of a concentrated hatch of mayflies, caddisflies, or stoneflies. Most stonefly nymphs are available to trout because they must lead an exposed life and are constantly on the move preying on other aquatic insects or being dislodged from their holds.

Big goldens are most common in the East during the first two months of summer, as is the case (with notable exceptions) in western waters. At this time of the fishing season their twilight, night, or early-morning hatches will take place. Actual emergences are similar to those of all stoneflies. The nymphs crawl out of the stream before hatching into adults. The nymphs are available to the trout in the greatest concentrations before their actual emergences, and trout will then begin to cruise the shallows looking for them. When fishing between late in the evening and early morning, it is advisable to apply the same technique of close-to-the-bank fishing that we suggested for fishing the salmon-fly hatches. The angler will be pleasantly surprised at the action he will receive in such areas of the river. The hours between six A.M. and eleven A.M. are especially productive, as are the evening hours of twilight. Just after nightfall the phenomenon of natural drift occurs, where large numbers of stoneflies, as well as other insects, let go of their holds to redistribute themselves along the bottom of the stream. It is at such times that the heaviest brown trout prefer to feed. Their splashy and bombardmentlike riseforms are usually the most reliable indications that they are eagerly hunting large stonefly species that are either drifting freely or emerging (as in the case of the big golden types). Adult activity, however, is always obvious and becomes specifically important when it takes place during the daylight hours (which is mainly the case with late-morning big goldens). This is especially true during days that begin with a heavy overcast. Activity begins again at dusk, when the adults of the eastern species, such as *P. capitata* and *P. media,* or of the western *A. pacifica,* complete the life cycle. At such times, the dry-fly pattern given later in this chapter should come to good use.

Fishing the dry patterns during the egg-laying phase of the large stoneflies can provide exciting angling, since the naturals are clumsy and easily become entangled in the surface film, unable to become airborne again. Presenting an imitation in the manner of the true natural (fluttering vio-

Hen-winged golden stone

Deer-hair golden stone

lently) will often result in violent rises. However, as we have already pointed out on numerous occasions, close observation of the behavior of the natural is the best clue to the angler on how he should present his artificial. The trick is to make the trout take an imitation confidently because it has both the *look* and *movement* of the natural.

Medium Browns and Yellows (Family Perlodidae)

The group of medium-size stoneflies classified by entomologists under this family heading (as well as those in the family Chloroperlidae, which follows) are important primarily in their adult stages. The activities of these stages include times when the adults are blown back onto the water during their emergence, and during the more common and reliable egg-laying phase of the life cycle. It is during the egg-laying phase that trout consume these winged stoneflies with the same deliberate riseform they use when feeding on the spent adults (or spinners) of mayflies and caddisflies. It is hard to appreciate the numbers in which the medium and small stoneflies of summer actually inhabit our trout streams. The life cycle of members of the families Perlodidae and Chloroperlidae consist of nymph-

Midwestern brown nymph

al forms that remain well burrowed in the bottom of a stream until just before the spring. At this time, one can seine a river to find its many well-hidden occupants.

STREAMSIDE IDENTIFICATION

The nymph of the family Perlodidae is obvious to the naked eye when encountered in the stream. It is easily recognized by its distinct markings. Two principal types that make up this family are the genera *Isogenus* and *Isoperla*. The great majority of *Isogenus* exhibit horizontal markings that run across their abdominal segments, while *Isoperla* nymphs have longitudinal lines on their abdomens. In general configuration they are distinct as well as being distinct in their markings. The upper, or first set, of wing pads are always at an angle to their bodies, with the apexes pointing away from their abdomen. The second set of wing pads have their apexes pointing parallel to the body. Unlike the similar-size early-season stoneflies discussed in Chapter Two, members of the family Perlodidae are patterned and not uniform in color. The inner notches in the wing pads are missing, while these notches are quite evident in the species of family Chloroperlidae, which we will discuss shortly. Perlodidae adults, at first glance, appear as miniature versions of the big goldens, ranging in basic coloration from chocolate brown to olive brown, with variably colored thoraxes. However, this stonefly also has pale lemon-yellow members that differ from some of the adults of the family Chloroperlidae by size alone.

EASTERN AND MIDWESTERN MEDIUM BROWNS AND YELLOWS

Perhaps no other family of stoneflies comes in so many different sizes and general forms than the Perlodidae. This makes it necessary to isolate and discuss certain distinct species in order to simplify imitation. In the East and Midwest, one type of *Isogenus* that stands out from the rest is *Isogenus olivaceous*. The adults of this handsome stonefly are commonly encountered during May and early June in many waters. In true early-season custom, it is often a midday emerger, and it is frequently noticeable because of its size, which causes otherwise lethargic trout to take the large, fluttering adults with vicious rises. Trout will rise the same way as they do when they snatch the large flies of the big goldens. In past seasons, we have encountered this rather large species more than the other members of its family. They emerge from many of the freestone streams of Pennsylvania, New York, and New England, as well as the smoothly flowing streams of the Midwest. The species, however, is not a very profuse emerger wherever found, but what it lacks in numbers it makes up for in a size that causes trout to respond reliably. The angler may expect their sporadic hatches during heavily overcast days in late spring, a perfect time to put the pattern we recommend for this species to use.

More common and dependable are the thick hatches of the olive-brown and medium-size stoneflies. *Isoperla bilineata* is of specific importance to the fly fisher, not only during the customary nocturnal emergence (ten P.M. to midnight), but during the evening egg-laying flight of the olive-brown females. In a fashion consistent with all adult types of stoneflies that belong to this family, this group has a suicidal manner of egg-laying. The females literally dive-bomb into the stream (and frequently onto freshly black-topped roads near streams) and then proceed to hop over and over again in an effort to deposit all their eggs in one attempt. Though they do not actually fall spent on the water, it takes them so long to lay their eggs that they become a tantalizing and exciting morsel for the trout.

A splashy riseform is the best streamside indication that this large, fluttering stonefly is on the water. The pattern that we suggest for this common stonefly is tied with hackle wound palmer style, because the fisherman must bounce and skip his imitation over the water to imitate the behavior of the natural. Unknowing anglers let their imitations float placidly and unnaturally along the drift lanes of the surface with little if any luck.

In general appearance *Isogenus decisus* and *Isoperla signata* differ radically from both of the types we have mentioned above. These two species are primarily the common pale-yellow stoneflies that emerge during summer months in eastern parts of the country. Both are found in all types of wa-

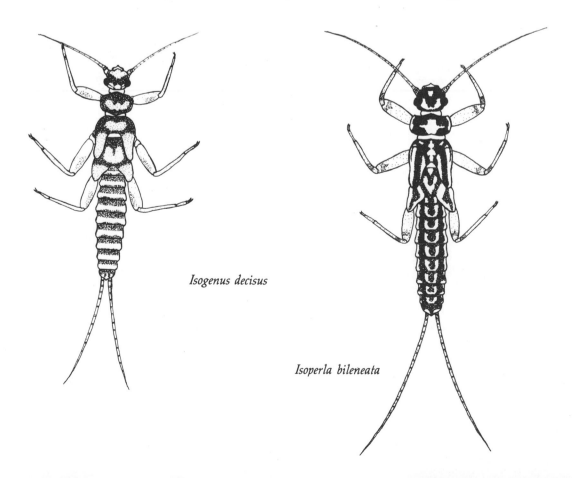

Isogenus decisus

Isoperla bileneata

ter, from fast freestone rivers to smooth-flowing, meandering rivers. In general biology, especially in their manner of egg-laying, they closely resemble the slightly larger olive-brown *I. bilineata.* In fact, these two species are so much like *I. bilineata* that the activities and manner of presentation mentioned for *I. bilineata* may apply to these two species as well.

WESTERN MEDIUM BROWNS AND YELLOWS

Trout waters west of the Mississippi River system have ample populations of both types that make up this family of common stoneflies, but in the West *Isoperla* are much more common than *Isogenus.* In the West the unusually large types, such as the *I. olivaceous* found in the East, are missing. Most western species are basically quite similar in size and coloration. This keeps the need for different artificial patterns to a minimum.

The medium-size, olive-brown types are formed by two ubiquitous species found in western waters: *Isoperla fulva* and *Isogenus tostonus.* Both are found in various types of waters. However, *I. fulva* is mainly responsible for the medium-brown activities found early in the season (June 1 to July 15) in medium- to fast-running streams and rivers. We have encountered

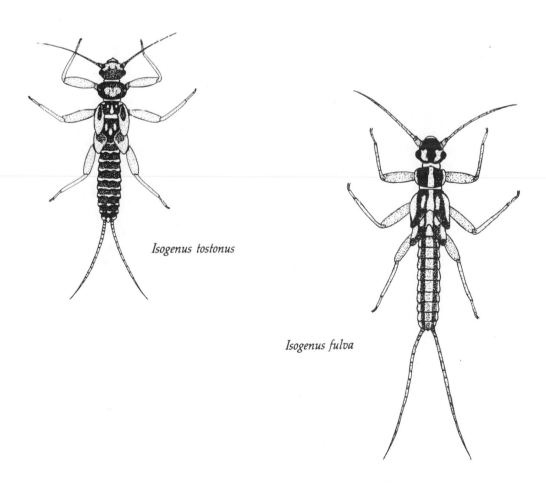

Isogenus tostonus

Isogenus fulva

their hatching and egg-laying activities from the rivers of California, such as the Owens before the spring runoff, to the trout waters of the Yellowstone Park area. They are even well represented in many Colorado rivers. *Isogenus tostonus* is a common stonefly that appears later in the season, lasting until late August. This species can be found in slow-moving waters and even in heavily silted waters that are more ideally suited for burrowing mayflies (*Ephemera*) and large, slow-water caddisflies (*Discomcoues* and *Limnephilus*). We found this stonefly from the Black Hills to the rivers of Montana, such as the Clarks Fork and the Beaverhead, south to rivers in the northern parts of Arizona and New Mexico.

In the West, the pale-yellow type of summer stonefly (commonly called the Yellow Sally) is comprised of two very common types of stonefly species: *Isoperla patricia* and *Isoperla mormona* (the latter name reflecting the common name Mormon Girl given to this stonefly). The former species, *I. patricia,* is much more in evidence to the angler. Making a distinction between the two species is superfluous, for both species are nearly identical in their adult stages, which are the stages of principal importance to the angler, and both appear to prefer the same type of water. They are often found emerging together. These are the conspicuous yellow stoneflies that

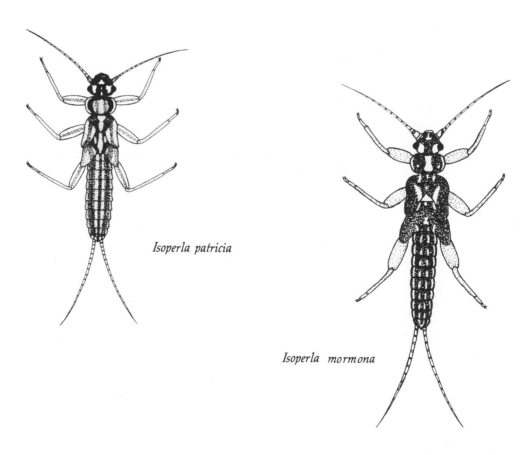

Isoperla patricia

Isoperla mormona

are quite common in western waters during the latter half of the season, from late June until well into September. The type of waters that they inhabit most frequently and abundantly are rivers like the Clarks Fork and the Big Hole in southwestern Montana, Henrys Fork in Idaho, and many of the slower streams in the Black Hills, Colorado, Arizona, New Mexico, and California.

FISHING THE MEDIUM BROWNS AND YELLOWS

The manner of emergence of the Perlodidae is typical of other stoneflies, and in true summer fashion it tends to take place in the earlier morning hours (eight A.M. to ten A.M.) when the temperature of the water is in the low 50-degree range. They precede the emergence of mayflies and caddisflies that emerge in late morning at that time of year. Some species, however, such as *Isogenus bilineata,* are nocturnal and don't start to emerge until two hours after dark. The hatching usually takes place on rocks near the stream, with the newly emerged adults traveling as much as ten to twenty feet before seeking cover.

Since these stoneflies, as is the case with the other summer types, do not feed as adults, their female egg-laying flight occurs within a few days of emergence. While they sometimes emerge in the morning, it is also common for them to hatch toward late afternoon or at dusk. Their enticing

Western yellow nymph

A nice western rainbow taken on a little green stonefly.

fluttering, caused by their method of ovipositing—gliding onto the water and then bouncing a few times before shaking off all the eggs—is a winning manner with hungry trout. It is our opinion that the best action takes place during late afternoon on days with cloud cover, or toward dusk during hot, bright days. It should be remembered that early in the season when days are cool and there is frequent cloud cover, their hatches and adult egg-laying activity will take place toward midday. This is to the advantage of the fly fisher who is accustomed to being on the stream at this time to encounter the hatches of mayflies and caddisflies.

Many of the species live in rapid, cool trout streams, but many forms, some of which are of great importance to the angler and are included here, are also equally at home in slow-flowing, meandering rivers of a type not usually associated with stoneflies.

The Little Yellows and Greens (Family Chloroperlidae)

The small, conspicuous adults of Family Chloroperlidae are the most important in either a hatch or spinner-fall situation from the middle to the end of summer, though they become evident in trout streams and rivers as early as May in the East and June in the West. In a most general sense, they make their first seasonal appearances right after the larger medium browns and yellows begin their seasonal hatches. Often the two types can be seen together in the same stretch of water, simultaneously emerging or ovipositing.

STREAMSIDE IDENTIFICATION

The general shape of the little nymphs of Chloroperlidae is thin and tubular, which must be advantageous to their manner of remaining well buried in the bottom until just before their emergence. In many waters they appear as if from nowhere and then become extremely abundant. Both types, or genera, that make up this family, have rounded wing pads that are parallel to the abdomen. The pads appear as if a section was clipped from an otherwise perfectly rounded wing pad. They are basically uniform in color, and unlike the nymphal forms of the stoneflies we have previously discussed, they lack any distinct markings. *Alloperla* are undoubtedly the most common and largest of the two types, in excess of 7mm, while *Chloroperla* are less than 7mm. The former types have notched inner margins in their wing pads, while *Chloroperla* have wing pads with straight inner margins, lacking the noticeable notch.

Adults of the Chloroperlidae are the smallest of the summer stoneflies, averaging 7 to 10mm in length (#18–14 hooks), and are the lightest in col-

Midwestern little
yellow nymph

oration, ranging from lemon yellow to bright green. A precise scientific distinction especially useful to separate the adults of Chloroperlidae from those of Perlodidae is the fact that they have a fork in the A_2 vein of the forewing indicated outside of the anal cell.

Consistent with the summer fauna, members of Chloroperlidae are sporadic emergers, but because of their pale coloring they are better adapted to emerge during daylight hours than are the darker stoneflies. From eight A.M. to ten A.M. is the best time to find them hatching. Their discarded nymphal shucks are often present in tremendous numbers, and it is a wonder how a trout stream can support their great abundance. Like the tiny winter blacks, of which they are a pale variation, they emerge at about midday. Many species lack wings, and in emerging the males procede the females. The adults of certain species resort to crawling migrations to compensate for the natural drift that occurs during the rest of the year.

The greatest adult activity (which is important to the angler) occurs toward late afternoon or evening, and again the time depends on cloud cover. The females appear from high in the trees, making a long descent toward the stream. Then they glide into the surface film and bounce a few times in rapid succession to extrude their eggs. The last hop is usually fatal, and they are so exhausted that they flop on the surface, similar to the behavior of mayfly spinners, and become available to the trout. It is a fascinating sight to see their great numbers lying spent on the water with trout making porpoiselike rises as they would for any easily obtained, helpless insect. When angling, this activity should be treated like a mayfly spinner fall, for in general these spent stoneflies have the same delta-wing configuration of the caddisflies.

Western Mormon girl

Our records are filled with encounters with the *Alloperla* on the trout streams of the Northeast, the Midwest, and almost every trout stream in the West that we have either seined or selected for observing hatches. Their range is extensive, and they are present in many different types of water. Classic freestone streams in the Green Mountains of Vermont offered us a lot of action on the *Alloperla.* The Catskill and Pocono waters have had a consistent occurrence of them for all the years we have fished those rivers. The West has produced superb hatches, not only in every trout stream of Montana, Idaho, Wyoming, and Colorado that we have fished, but in the numerous steelhead rivers along the Pacific Coast during the fall as well. Those hatches in Oregon, from the Chetco south to northern California, in particular have impressed us.

EASTERN AND MIDWESTERN LITTLE YELLOWS AND GREENS

Due to the similarity of the species in both the nymphal and adult stages, it is not necessary to make a separation between these species. Besides, the greatest hatches consist of only two species: *Alloperla caudata,* a common delicate yellow species, and *Alloperla imbecilla,* a conspicuous bright green species. Other lesser species produce either the yellow or green versions throughout the summer, and for this reason we suggest tying the pattern given in Chapter Seven in both colors.

WESTERN LITTLE YELLOWS AND GREENS

Our research found the Chloroperlidae species to be much more common in western waters than in eastern and midwestern waters. *Alloperla pallidula,* a common and delicate yellow species, become quite frequent in most creeks and rivers from July through September. They show in terrific

Little olive hairwing

Little yellow and green

populations as late as October in many steelhead waters in the Pacific states. Many lakes show populations, where the flies become prevalent along the shores at night. The imitation given later is most effective for cruising trout in such waters. The nymphs have a discernable stripe along the abdomen and U-shaped markings on the thoracic segments. We found them in the big Yellowstone, from the park waters to its junction with the Musselshell below Livingston, but they are equally at home in small rivers as well. *Alloperla coloradensis* is another yellow species with excellent hatches in many of the intermountain areas. Rivers such as the Madison in Montana and the Roaring Fork in Colorado have given us much action with these stoneflies during July. *Alloperla pacifica,* whose emergence takes place later in the season, are equally abundant during August and can be found as far west as California. They are present in California's Hat Creek and many of the river systems that drain either side of the Sierras.

The western green stoneflies may be represented by *Alloperla delicata,* with its delicate, bright green adults most common in the northern Rocky Mountain states such as Montana and Idaho. They are also abundant in the Pacific Northwest. It is interesting to note that it also has a yellow phase, and so it is almost identical to species mentioned above. Its numbers are evident rather early in the season, during June and July. *A. severa* is another of the little green stoneflies that is important in the adult stage in the Rocky Mountain states. We have encountered its excellent concentrations at the same time as those of *A. delicata,* during June and July, in such Wyoming trout streams as the Shoshone and nearby streams, and, in Montana, the Yellowstone below Gardiner (stations 5 and 6), and in many trout streams of Colorado, such as the Gunnison and the lower Frying Pan past Ruedi. Both of these species make up the green stonefly types in each section of the West, and they are hard to confuse with those of any other species.

We should mention two stonefly species that belong to the family of the Medium Browns and Yellows and the Little Yellows and Greens: *Arcynopteryx parallela* and *Paraperla frontalis*. Both are unusually large, considering the proportions of other member species with which they are classified, and are a dark golden-brown. Consequently, both are well imitated by the Big Golden patterns given in Chapter Seven. These two species customarily make their appearance in western trout streams between April and June, usually before spring run off. Because of their early seasonal occurence and their comparatively large size, they may turn out to be of great local importance to western anglers. Their best populations are found in western Montana and northern Idaho, and they become quite numerous in certain trout streams and steelhead rivers of the Pacific Coast. The experiences that we had with their emergences were confined to the tributaries of the San Joaquin and Sacramento river systems of California, the large to medium-flowing rivers of Idaho—such as the Lochsa and the Bitteroot—and the Clarks Fork and Smith rivers in Montana. However, we do suspect these two stoneflies to be of consequence in many other trout waters. In all situations, their early-to-late-morning hatches gave us good activity when employing a $1/_4$-inch-long nymph fished very close to shore. Their numbers completely disappear from western trout streams by the middle of June.

A Favorite Dry Stonefly Pattern

One of our favorite flies for medium and small stoneflies is easy to tie and quite realistic in appearance. It complements the specific prototypical patterns given in Chapter Seven. It can be used as an imitation for any family when tied in the appropriate size and color. It can also be used as a general type to imitate any species, using exact shades of colors for any species the angler may find common on his favorite waters.

TAILS: Two fibers from a primary duck wing, tied short and spread wide

BODY: Spun fur of appropriate shade, tied on ⅔ of the shank from bend to hook eye to leave plenty of room for hackle and wings

HACKLE: One top-quality cock hackle, clipped off top of hook shank after being wound to leave room for wing

WING: Two hen hackle or hen body feathers of appropriate color for species of stonefly being imitated. These are moistened with a good-quality nail polish and tied flat over the body after the hackle has been wound and clipped on top

Later, when on the stream, if the fisherman needs a pattern that lies flush on the surface, he may clip the hackle fibers off the bottom.

The Albino Nymph

Most of the big goldens and the smaller, lighter-colored stoneflies have medium-brown nymphs. But just after the nymphs have shed their skins,

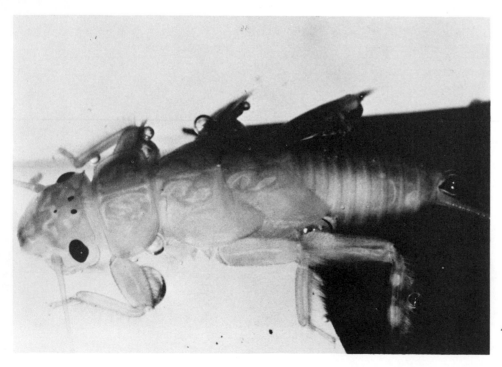

Albino—new instar

which enables them to grow (a new instar), they look like an albino. They are a very light cream with tan ribbing and have light tan to cream wing cases. Trout seem to prefer this stage much like a bass prefers a soft rather than a hard-shelled crayfish. We can imitate the fresh instar by using any of the good nymph patterns given later, but in the colors mentioned above. This does not work with the big black stoneflies, such as *Pteronarcys* and other very dark species, because they are only slightly lighter at the new instar stage. However, the albino-nymph imitation works extremely well for the little yellow and green stonefly nymphs.

Albino nymph *J. Frederic Oswalt*

CHAPTER FIVE

Stonefly Tackle, Techniques, and Tactics

IN THIS CHAPTER WE PROVIDE INFORMATION ON TACKLE, TECHNIQUES AND TACTICS that will aid the angler when fishing stonefly imitations. For the most part we limit our discussion to those aspects that pertain to fishing stonefly imitations. However, there is some general information in the sections that follow, and we hope the angler will find much in this chapter that is applicable to fishing imitations of trout-stream insects other than stoneflies.

Tackle

As a rod material, graphite has been developed about as far as we can go with it. It is doubtful that we could develop rod blanks with over 5 percent more efficient actions than the blanks we have today, and probably less than 1 percent of our present-day fly casters could take advantage of or even notice the slight improvement. The greatest advantages of graphite over fiberglass and bamboo as a rod material are *reduced weight* and *greater sensitivity*. Reduced weight is a result of the fact that graphite fibers are stiffer than are the fibers of most other rod materials, so fewer fibers are used in construction. This is a tremendous advantage in long rods. Fewer fibers also mean less mass in the rod, which results in more sensitivity, or better feel. A force applied at the tip of a rod, as when fighting a fish or when striking a fish while nymphing, tends to dissipate itself as it travels toward the butt, or grip end. Lighter rods with less mass retain more of this transmitted force, resulting in greater sensitivity. (This last point is illustrated by the overwhelming popularity of the graphite casting rods used by bass fishermen, where feel is critical to fish the plastic worm successfully.)

Boron, a new rod material, is developing about the way that graphite was coming along several years ago. Currently, a little more design work is needed in boron rods to reduce breakage and improve action. Modern, higher-priced fiberglass (sometimes called "S-glass" or high-density fiberglass) is a good second choice to graphite. These rods may be a little heavier and less sensitive than graphite rods, but good actions are available. Most bamboo rods are a bit too flexible or sloppy in action to throw tight, wind-penetrating loops and give the good control we like to have, especially when fishing large stonefly patterns. Even bamboo with the better, or stiffer, action has more mass than graphite and results in heavy and less sensitive rods.

Improved rods may result eventually from the blending of two or more materials, producing rods from fiberglass-and-graphite or boron-and-graphite composites. As modern plastics are developed we will see stronger and lighter rods evolve.

The next major improvement in fly rods should be in the guides. Anglers have been stuck with the inefficiencies of snake guides and pear-shaped tip-top guides for years. Round or oval shapes are far superior because they greatly reduce the friction in medium and long casts and aid in feeding the line out through the guides when fishing downstream. Probably the deadliest technique in dry-fly fishing is the downstream float, and to do this efficiently, the line must flow smoothly out of the guides without dragging the fly.

Most of our stonefly angling is done with a high-visibility, weight-forward, floating fly line. Bright chartreuse lines are a great aid, especially in some of the murky-water situations early in the year when the salmon flies are on. It has been scientifically proven that chartreuse shows up to the human eye better than any other color, especially in dim-light situations. This is why the bright, yellowish green tennis balls are so popular. The fishing is usually best during times of low light: early morning, late evening, and cloudy days. It is a great aid to one's fishing technique to be able to see his line on or in the water. It's particularly good for detecting strikes when nymphing—far more effective than the bright indicator tip that some anglers have been using over the past years.

Weight-forward lines are practical for the big water where we normally fish stonefly imitations. These lines enable us to make long casts and turn over large, wind-resistant imitations. It is best to use floating lines whenever possible, because they have a better hooking angle, and they can be mended and manipulated better than sinking-tip or sinking lines. They are

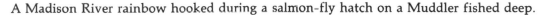

A Madison River rainbow hooked during a salmon-fly hatch on a Muddler fished deep.

also easier to pick up off the water. A weight-forward, sinking-tip line is a good back-up line for special deep-water situations. A sinking-tip line is much better than a full-sinking line, because the floating section behind the sinking tip retains some of the hooking, mending, and picking-up qualities of a floating line.

High-visibility, flat-butt leaders extend our high-visibility system to within a couple of feet of the fly and have about everything one would want in a leader. They have great turnover and ease of straightening with just hand pressure (no leather or rubber patches needed). They have excellent visibility, and because of the flat-butt design the connection to the fly line can be made with a three-turn nail knot that leaves a very short, small-diameter connection. The connection to a permanent monofilament butt section can be made with a two-turn blood knot. This also leaves a very small knot in the system. Either of these connections flows through the guides easily. Tippets are clear, strong, and they don't kink.

Using split-shot and Twistons (small, flat lengths of lead that can be wrapped onto the leader) has been the standard method of adding weight to a leader for sinking a fly deep, but the new lead sleeves that are available are far superior to anything we have ever tried. They have reduced air resistance for ease of casting and reduced water resistance for quicker sinking. Most big fish, especially during the salmon-fly hatch, are along the banks under tag alders, willows, or other overhanging cover. With lead sleeves the angler can cast a much tighter loop to put the fly effectively under these obstructions than he can with split-shot or Twistons. With split-shot it's almost impossible to throw a loop narrow enough to get into these tight places. Once in the water, lead sleeves sink quicker because their slim, elongated shape offers much less water resistance than the other types of weight. We've often used as many as six sleeves on a leader and still have been able to cast a decent loop. With this many split-shot,

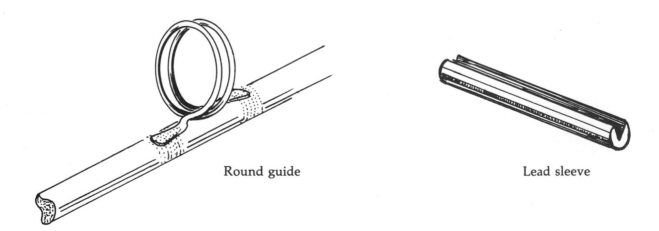

Round guide   Lead sleeve

control is almost impossible. The first sleeve is usually pinched on about eighteen inches above the fly, with successive sleeves being spaced up the leader every two or three inches. They are easily attached and removed.

When fishing stoneflies deep in heavy water we sometimes use weighted nymphs, although we try to use unweighted imitations as much as possible. The heavier the artificial, the less it will act like the natural in the current. In especially heavy currents, lead-core shooting-tapers and the new Hi-Speed Hi-D fast-sinking line from Scientific Anglers can be used to get the fly to the bottom. When using this type of fast-sinking line, the angler should use a short leader and fish down and across so the fly comes to the fish before the line and leader. The short leader doesn't allow the fly to swing much higher than the line in the water.

The angler should be sure to cast wide loops when there is a lot of weight in the system. If he tries to throw too tight a loop with split-shot, Twistons, or lead sleeves the line will tangle. The rule is: the greater the weight, the wider the loop.

Techniques

Many of the standard dry-fly and nymph strategies for fishing mayfly and caddisfly imitations are effective when applied to stoneflies, but there are some specialized techniques that are often more effective. These techniques take into consideration the unique emergence behavior of the Plecoptera and the egg-laying flights of what are often large, fluttering insects.

Typical float fishing during the salmon-fly hatch

Perhaps the most effective method of fishing the hatches of the huge salmon flies on our western rivers is floating. Float-fishing presents some problems that are not normally encountered with any other method. The fly, be it a nymph or adult imitation, must be cast accurately, usually under bushes, trees, and other obstructions. The cast must be made as far under these obstructions and as close to the bank as possible. The angler must somehow achieve a drag-free float, at least for a few feet, and all this must be accomplished in fast, crisscross currents while the caster and the boat are moving. And it must be done correctly the first time, because the fisherman usually doesn't get a second chance. None of this is easy, but those who have mastered the technique are often rewarded with large catches of fine fish.

The dry fly must float well and be reusable in the turbulent currents. The nymphs must be fished near the bottom but must not drag furiously through the current. Good casting and good equipment are essential. One of the most effective and necessary skills to be mastered for float-fishing is the "reach cast." It is an accurate cast and produces long, drag-free floats under difficult conditions. No other cast can duplicate its effect, and it comes into good use in many situations besides float-fishing.

The reach cast enables the angler to lay the belly of the line upstream or downstream from him, depending on the current, so he gets the longest drag-free float he can. Reach casts are much more effective than slack-line casts; they give longer floats and are more accurate. The caster is at the mercy of the wind with a slack-line cast, because it is formed in the air and must fall down to the water. On a windy day it is almost impossible to control. The reach cast, being a straight-line cast, is a power cast and can be thrown with tea-cup accuracy even in a high wind. During a hatch of large stoneflies, such as the salmon flies, imitations must be cast in under overhanging cover along the banks. The reach cast is the most effective tool for these tough situations.

During the power stroke of the reach cast the angler changes the direction of the rod tip 90 degrees. That is, he starts with the rod tip pointing directly at the target and ends up with the rod tip pointing either right or left. If the power is applied *evenly*, a beautiful, straight-line cast will result, with the fly, the leader and the line hitting the water at approximately the same time. If the fly flutters down late, the power was not applied properly. With a little practice an angler can throw the cross-body reach cast (a left reach for right-handers) with great accuracy under almost any overhanging obstacle.

When fishing downstream the angler must have the ability to feed the fly line quickly and efficiently out through the rod guides. This allows long, drag-free floats and provides excellent presentations. With this method the fly comes in to the fish's window of vision first, eliminating

Beginning the reach cast to the left—the first two positions

The third position of the reach cast

the possibility of lining the trout (or spooking it by casting the line and/or leader over it). To learn this technique properly, the fisherman must practice transferring the line from his line-handling hand to underneath the index finger of his rod hand. This forms a small, hanging loop of line between the first stripping guide and the rod grip. Then, without moving his arm, the angler snaps his casting wrist vertically, and the line will jump

The final position of the reach cast

Reach cast to the right

out through the guides. If the angler keeps repeating this procedure, he will quickly learn how to pay out line evenly without affecting the drift of the fly.

Repositioning the line on the water is called mending and is usually done for one of three reasons: to take tension out of the line-and-leader system so a nymph will sink; to reduce or eliminate drag on a dry fly; or to create a track (or path) to swim a streamer or nymph through. Few anglers have mastered mending, mainly because they never practice. To develop this technique, the angler must learn to move the line into new positions on the water either by snapping his rod-hand wrist or quickly rolling the rod-hand wrist. The quicker the movement, the more the rod loads, which results in more efficient mending. Most anglers make the mistake of using too much arm and too little wrist when mending line.

To fish a stonefly nymph deep the angler must learn to mend the leader and line into a position directly behind, or upstream from, the fly. If he

Feeding line

can get the fly, leader, and line positioned in the same line of drift, the nymph will sink. The problem with most anglers is that they mend the leader and line into *different* veins of current. This keeps tension on the fly, and it won't sink. Most fisherman fail at nymphing because they don't know exactly *where* to mend, or if they know where to mend they don't have the ability to do it properly. Once again, mastering this technique is mainly a matter of practice. The correct mend for most situations is a very tight-angle mend. That is, the leader and line should be "stacked in" just behind the fly. This requires a lot of practice to do properly. The wrist must be rolled around in such a way that line is shot out toward the target. It is easy to mend at right angles to the direction of a cast, but it is much more difficult to "stack-mend" at angles of 10 or 20 degrees behind the fly. With a little practice, however, it can be mastered.

Quite often, to imitate the movements of the stonefly adults, we must skitter or twitch our imitations. The first step when using these techniques is to make sure that the entire system—fly, leader, and line—is floating properly. Dry flies should be dipped in Scotchguard (a waterproofing treatment) and then treated with floatant at the stream. Floatant should also be applied to the leader and the first thirty feet of fly line to skitter or twitch the imitation properly.

Skittering is one of the few fly-fishing techniques that requires a high rod position. With the rod held almost vertical, the angler should strip the line in under the index finger of the rod hand, and at the same time cause the rod tip to vibrate with the same hand. If the stripping and vibrating motions are coordinated perfectly and done with lightninglike flicks, any

Stack mending

Skittering

high-floating fly can be skittered or twitched across the current with amazing realism. This technique can be used to simulate a stonefly nymph crawling to shore when the angler is in a boat or wading in the middle of a river as well as being valuable for fishing an adult.

A big stonefly nymph does not crawl from shore to a deep riffle. Most anglers fish them in this unnatural manner. We devised a method that allows us to simulate the correct behavior of the natural, which crawls from the riffle toward shore, while positioned in the middle of the river. We cast a weighted nymph ten feet or so short of the shoreline from a position in or near the middle of the stream. Then we mend line so that a large loop is thrown beyond the fly, next to the shore. The current then will pull the mended loop of line in such a way that the nymph will crawl along the bottom toward the shoreline rather than away from it. This takes a little practice, as do the other techniques mentioned here, but the effort is well worth it.

Finally, on the matter of technique, if the angler encounters an especially hard-to-fool fish, he might try the following "game plan" to make the fish take. First, he should try a drag-free float over the trout. If that

Note how the large curve in the line leads the fly to move first toward the shore—which duplicates the way stonefly nymphs crawl toward shore to hatch.

doesn't work, he should try twitching the fly *before* it reaches the fish's window of vision, then allow it to drift quietly into the window. Next, he should try actively skittering the fly across the window. If the above methods fail to produce a take from the trout, the fisherman should drop the fly directly into the fish's window—that is, "hit the fish on the head."

Tactics

Fly-fishing with stonefly imitations can be divided into four main categories: dry-fly fishing to imitate the adult egg-laying flier; fishing the shoreward-migrating nymphs deep in the runs and pools or near the banks as they are crawling out; fishing the water when there is no great insect activity apparent; and night fishing for very big fish with both wet and dry imitations.

The larger stoneflies are like other large insects: flush hatches are elusive. It is seldom, for example, that the angler will come across huge flights of *Pteronarcys*. But they do occur, and when the angler finds them it's fantastic fishing. The tactic we use to locate the *Pteronarcys* hatches is also a basic technique for fishing almost all of the stonefly hatches.

When float-fishing to the salmon flies the idea is to launch the float boat upstream from any insect activity. When the boat comes into the first area that has a few discarded nymphal shucks on the rocks and logs by the banks, the fisherman is into the area where the nymphs are crawling out. Here, weighted nymphs fished on the bottom and crawled toward shore is the preferred technique. In the salmon-fly hatch this area of the nymphal appearance covers from one to three miles of river in most cases. Farther downstream is the area in which the adults are active, and here the fishing is with dry flies. Warm, windy afternoons are best for this kind of fishing. The angler should try both low-riding and high-riding imitations when fishing dry flies. The Bird's Stonefly pattern, described in Chapter Seven, is one of the best for the *Pteronarcys* adults, along with Mike Lawson's patterns that are mentioned in Chapter Three and are described in Chapter Seven also.

When the hatch is over in a particular section of stream the angler may get better results fishing to fish that are accustomed to feeding on these large, meaty morsels than he got during the hatch itself. The fish will be on the lookout for them. The trout can be quickly sated when the hatch is heavy, but later, when the insects are finished hatching, the fish may hit an artificial with more enthusiasm. Some of the best fishing can be at this time. There are usually a few stragglers among the stoneflies, so it is a good bet that the fish will be feeding on them.

Some of our favorite fishing is in June to a little #12 olive stonefly, late in the evening, on Michigan's Pere Marquette River. We use the same searching nymph and dry-fly tactic on this hatch, although we wade instead of float. The shucks on the banks tell us to what stretch of the river the hatch has progressed. The early brown stones of New York and Pennsylvania are daytime emergers to which the same tactic can be applied. The early brown stones also provide good selective feeding to dry flies on warm, early-spring afternoons. The tiny winter blacks can live some weeks after emergence, but the spring and summer species oviposit just a few days after hatching. If the angler sees the shucks of these spring and summer stoneflies, he can usually count on some good hatch activity rather quickly.

Stonefly imitations are often the deadliest patterns for luring very large, night-feeding brown trout. The naturals are quite often very large and provide a real mouthful for big fish. Both the large drys and the Squirrel

Tail series of wets (described in Chapter Seven) consistently produce the largest fish for us in eastern and midwestern waters. Though night fishing is not practical in the West, it is nevertheless the most effective tactic for catching big fish. Large rainbows and brooks as well as browns feed after dark. Warm, dark, muggy nights seem to be best. These conditions do not happen as often in the West as they do on our eastern and midwestern streams, but when they do they produce unbelievable angling.

From dark until the hours of first light, big goldens and brown stones are deadly. Some eastern species emerge between four A.M. and six A.M., when the angler usually has the river to himself. If he can drag himself out of a warm, cozy bed to fish these early hours, he may be rewarded with some of the largest fish in the stream.

When night fishing we use short casts. Fish on the prowl after dark are not nearly as shy as they are in daylight. We wade slowly and quietly and listen for sounds of large fish feeding. We use big dry patterns, large nymphs fished on the bottom, and the wet Squirrel Tails for barely subsurface fishing. We fish the shallows near the shoreline and the big flats at the tails of pools. Nymphs tied on Keel-type hooks reduce hangups, and these hooks are especially handy when using weighted nymphs after dark. Finally, we try to know the river bottom well when fishing at night. If necessary, we go to the area during daylight and explore. If the angler fishes a section of stream when he can see it well, he'll save himself much time and trouble when he fishes it at night.

One last thought on stonefly fishing: we have often found that it does not take a large flight of Plecoptera to produce a rise of fish, which is usually unlike the smaller mayflies and caddisflies. Many times only a few large stoneflies will be fluttering at dusk and occasionally hitting the water. It appears that good fish are almost always on the lookout for this, so on evenings that appear to be rather dull it pays to fish the water with a big black or big golden imitation.

One night, just after full dark, we were fishing the Pere Marquette. We heard what sounded like very large fish jumping out of the river and falling back with a loud splash. We had never encountered this kind of behavior before, and at first we could not figure out what was happening. We finally got so curious that we took out our flashlights and aimed them at the area where the strange noises were coming from. There were a few huge, black *Pteronarcys* adults dipping over a riffle at the head of a pool, and large browns were jumping as much as a foot out of the water after them. We watched this pool for a few minutes, tied on some big, dark, fluttering stonefly imitations, and had one of the most productive evenings imaginable. We have since found that this type of fishing in the late spring and early summer is not unusual, and if the angler knows what to look for he can discover it quite often. The finding is worth the seeking.

CHAPTER SIX

Stoneflies and Atlantic Salmon

ON OUR FIRST TRIP TO THE UNGAVA BAY WATERSHED WE DISCOVERED SOME VERY interesting things about Atlantic salmon.

Atlantic salmon love stoneflies, the dry variety, not the nymphs, and the higher-floating the better. The reasons, upon reflection, seem perfectly logical. After all, the type of streams Atlantic salmon are usually found in is perfect habitat for large stoneflies, and the years that the immature salmon spend in the home water before going to sea must entail many meals of natural stoneflies.

If it is true, as is often suggested, that one of the prime triggering mechanisms for an adult salmon's rise is the "remembrance" of its parr life and the food it fed on as a parr, then stoneflies would appear to be a normal thing and perhaps one of the primary triggering mechanisms to induce the adult salmon to rise. At any rate, a well-designed artificial is deadly. It is now generally accepted that adult salmon do rise to natural insects, and, of course, anyone who has fished for them knows that they do hit artificial dry flies. Whether they actually swallow the natural flies and digest them

An Atlantic salmon
taken on a dry stonefly

is debatable. However, we and many other people have observed adult salmon rising to a hatch of natural insects. In fact, no less an authority than Lee Wulff wrote us a little while ago saying that after doing some research on the Delay River (a tributary of the Koksowak) in the Ungava Bay region of northern Quebec, he observed adult salmon, some of them black salmon (spawned-out fish), feeding on a great spinner flight of large, dark stoneflies in July. Lee states in the *Atlantic Salmon Journal* (the publication of the International Atlantic Salmon Foundation) that his most effective fly for big fish (large Atlantic salmon) is the Surface Stonefly, which is similar to the Bomber or the Muddler. He reasons that the stonefly has a stronger imprint on the salmon mind as a parr than other insects do and is more likely to trigger a response in a big fish that has had a longer time at sea to "forget" the more minor insects.

A few years ago, we started fishing this same region of subarctic Quebec, primarily the Whale and the George rivers. This area is perhaps one of the last relatively unexploited salmon areas, many parts of it yet to be explored. Of course, Atlantic-salmon fishing is normally extremely expensive, and with disease in the British Isles and the netting on the high seas, which has hurt some of the European stocks, plus the netting in the estuaries off Norway, we believe the Ungava region is the best Atlantic-salmon fishing area today. It is especially so if you consider three things: cost, average size of fish, and average number of fish caught. The cost was within our reach; the average size of the fish was about fourteen pounds (with few grilse taken); and the average number of fish caught for a competent fly caster was between fifteen and twenty-five fish in a seven-day period.

This area and its salmon runs do not seem to change much from season to season. Perhaps a maximum of a three-week difference in the peak of the run is all that has been noticeable to us.

The river is fed mostly by snowmelt, and the fish usually come in whether it rains or not, though high water is best. Since we could not afford to take a week or two off to visit another area, where we might miss the run completely or hit in the middle of a drought and perhaps catch nothing or only a few grilse, this area seemed to us to be ideal. It is not inexpensive, but also not as outrageously expensive as Iceland or Norway.

The first year we fished the area, we visited the Helen Falls Camp on the George. This spot was recommended to us by Everett Kertcher, owner of Boyne Mountain and Big Sky ski resorts, who holds the record fish on the George. He told us the fish were good size, with sea lice still clinging to the salmon fresh from the sea. On top of that they seemed to prefer dry flies. He had caught them the year before on a huge Paradrake imitation similar to the patterns that we had used in the Midwest to imitate the large *Hexagenia limbata* mayfly dun.

Our Eskimo guide took us upriver about two miles to the salmon lies and spotted us at our assigned pools. They told us any fly was fine, as long as it was black (their favorite is a Black Mink-tail Green-Butt), and it should be fished with a Portland hitch (or riffling hitch). What they were actually recommending was a standard dark hairwing salmon fly, fished in the film with a swimming or dragging action, much like skittering a dry fly. There was no doubt that it was an effective pattern and technique, taking many fish over the week. We had, however, come here with the idea of trying dry flies for Atlantic salmon, and what the majority of the anglers were actually doing was skating wet flies in the manner of swimming a large stonefly, though they did not think of it in that way. Dave Whitlock, at our suggestion, had tied us a variety of stonefly imitations from small, black, #10 *Brachyptera* patterns to giant, #4, 3XL *Pteronarcys* types. We reasoned that this river was such a big, brawling, tumbling, boulder-strewn river that it must be ideal habitat for large stoneflies.

Most of the anglers at the camp would not carry and did not try dry flies, probably because it was not traditional, and dry flies were not considered as effective as the other recommended patterns. The guides did not suggest drys, the trip was expensive, and they were there for such a short time that the anglers did not really want to spend time experimenting.

The George River at Helen Falls

They wanted to use something that they were absolutely sure would be as effective as possible.

After that first week of fishing the slick salmon pools of the Helen Falls Camp, we found the dry stoneflies were at least as effective as the standard hairwing wet flies, and we were convinced they were a great deal more effective. They were certainly more fun to fish.

In later years we learned that some of the knowledgeable anglers who have come back year after year to fish this area use dry flies and large dry concoctions, such as Bombers (which probably imitate stoneflies), at least 80 percent of the time. In fact, the "meat fishermen" (there are a few even on salmon streams) have found drys to be more effective and use them most of the time. The fish prefer to come up to take and will rarely take a fly deep in the pool.

We have experimented quite a bit with stonefly nymphs and other wet-fly patterns fished very deep or crawling on the bottom and have found these generally to be worthless. Atlantic salmon seem to prefer to take an artificial in the area between two feet under the surface and the surface. In our experience the closer to the surface the fly swims the more effective it is. Why more people do not use dry flies for Atlantic salmon is somewhat of a mystery considering how deadly they are, and how much more interesting the fishing technique is to the angler. A lot has been written about dry-fly fishing for Atlantics, but one doesn't find many anglers actually doing it. (We should note, of course, that in some regions, such as Iceland, salmon will simply not take the dry fly regularly.)

Tackle

These rivers in the Ungava Bay area are extremely wide and deep. Most of the fishing is to the pools along the edges. It is possible to fish from the bank, or wading a little way out and casting toward the middle of the stream, or from a canoe. In some cases the best lies can only be reached by fishing from a boat. It is traditional to fish some of the salmon pools exclusively by wading, however, and in either case the person with suitable equipment for distance casting and the ability to cast long distances has a decided advantage. If ten people are fishing at a salmon camp and two of the ten have the ability to cast beyond a hundred feet, whereas the other eight are only capable of casting forty to sixty feet, the two distance casters will present their flies to many more fish than the short casters and will present their flies to fresh fish that have not been cast over repeatedly. This is extremely important, for in Atlantic-salmon fishing, the fresher the fish, the easier it is to get him to take—as a general rule. Of course, on some of the smaller waters, such as the Icelandic rivers, where the pools are narrow, distance casting would not be important, and one could use

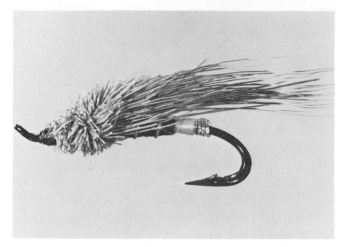

Jorgensen's Atlantic
salmon streaker

smaller, lighter rods. However, in the larger rivers that we have been fishing lately, graphite rods between 8 and $9\frac{1}{2}$ feet, taking a 7- to a 10-weight line, have completely taken over from the other materials, such as bamboo and fiberglass. The graphite rods are not only much lighter for the size of line they throw, but they are able to cast greater distances as well. Even a poor caster will be able to cast farther with a graphite rod than with a bamboo or fiberglass model. A 9-foot rod taking a 9- or a 10-weight line would be ideal for this kind of river. Also, even the smaller stonefly artificials are rather bulky and have quite a bit of air resistance, and the longer rods and heavier lines will turn them over much better than a smaller rod with a lighter line.

Any good salmon or saltwater fly reel will suffice; however, our favorite is the Fin Nor model #1 or model #2. If a 30-foot shooting-taper is used with 90 feet of flat monofilament shooting-line attached to 100 or 200 yards of 20-pound-test Dacron backing, more line can be held on the reel, and, of course, as much backing as possible is desirable. If a large salmon gets in the rapids and starts running downstream, the more backing the better.

The fly line should be a floating line. Sinking lines are not desirable in most cases in Atlantic-salmon fishing. The ideal fly line for dry-fly Atlantic-salmon fishing is the first 30 feet of a double-tapered fly line to which 90 feet of flat monofilament shooting-line is attached by a nail knot. The flat monofilament ties a neat, inconspicuous nail knot. It has little memory so it does not coil, and it shoots through the rod guides beautifully. If the shooting-line gets twisted, as it quite often does, the flat monofilament can be held between the fingers and stripped in, and it will untwist itself, because the flat monofilament will stay in one plane.

Most of the guides on these salmon rivers will tell an angler that it doesn't make any difference how heavy a leader he uses (many anglers use 20-pound test). In our experience, however, the lighter the leader the more rises one will get. Perhaps the ideal weight for the tippet would be 6- to 8-pound test, but the lighter the better—4-pound test does seem to get more strikes.

When the angler is playing big fish on fairly light leaders his knots are extremely important. We suggest using the improved blood knot for tying the last two tippet sections on the tapered leader. It is much stronger than a standard blood knot. An improved clinch knot to tie the fly on is also strong. Even on turned-down-eye or turned-up-eye hooks, the improved clinch knot is still the best. It is much stronger than a turle knot, which is often used.

Techniques

Atlantic-salmon take the dry stoneflies with a number of different rise-forms. There can be a dimple, and the fly will disappear. The fish can come clear out of the water and down on top of the fly. And often it appears as if a wall of water comes toward the fly, and the fly is engulfed. In most of these cases the tendency is to strike much too quickly. It is better to wait until the angler almost feels the fish, and then he should gently raise the rod tip. Once the angler feels the fish is hooked, then he can hit it a couple of times to make sure the hook penetrates. But he should be careful not to strike too soon.

In approaching a typical salmon slick the dry stonefly is cast a short distance upstream and allowed to float back downstream freestyle, or free-float, as in typical dry-fly fishing for trout during a rise. The cast is gradually lengthened until the entire holding area has been covered. If no fish has shown, the next thing to try is twitching the fly. The fly is cast upstream, and as it floats back, it is twitched, or popped, occasionally like a bass bug. About 50 percent of the fish that are taken will take on the dead float, and about 30 percent of the fish that refuse the dead float will take the popped fly. If the popped fly gets no response the fly should be cast up and across and allowed to swim in the manner that a wet fly is fished with a Portland hitch. The speed at which the fly should swim is important, as the fish seem to prefer the fly swimming at a constant speed. The exact swimming speed is something that the angler must find out for himself by trial and error or have someone on the stream who is knowledgeable demonstrate for him. It should not be too fast or too slow, but a gentle swimming motion. If the angler can envision the speed of a mouse swimming across the current, he will have it. If he can imagine this and make his fly swim at that same rate he will get more strikes. In fact, wet flies fished below the surface should swim at that same ideal speed. Of course, it's hard to tell how fast a wet fly is swimming because the fisherman can't see it, but if he gets some experience swimming a dry stonefly, then he can relate this to the same type of water and the same current speed and make his wet fly swim in the same manner. If the angler is fishing a slow pool, it is sometimes advisable to speed up the cast by stripping in gently with the left hand, imparting a constant acceleration to the fly. In very fast current it is sometimes advisable to let the line out with the left hand to slow the fly down. Salmon do not usually like a fly dragged through the water at an extremely rapid speed, nor do they like a fly drifting too slowly.

Dry Stonefly Patterns for Atlantic Salmon

Four prototypical patterns are listed here, each to represent important families of stoneflies found on salmon rivers.

THE TINY WINTER BLACK AND SPRING BROWNS (THE WINTER FAUNA)

These smaller imitations represent the winter and spring species of Capniidae, genera *Capnia* and *Allocapnia,* and family Taeniopterygidae, genera *Brachypteras* and *Taeniopteryx.*

HOOK:	#8–12, 3XL, TDE, light-wire Mustad streamer hook, or TUE, Mustad salmon dry-fly hook
THREAD:	black nymo or monocord
TAILS:	black hackle fibers
BODY:	black and/or dark brown spun fur or polypropylene yarn
WING:	light to medium-gray feather section, clipped to shape and tied flat over the back, treated with plastic cement
LEGS AND HEAD:	medium dark gray deer hair, clipped to shape with back fibers left long on sides to represent legs
HACKLE:	none

Atlantic salmon black adult

THE HUGE BLACKS (THE SALMON-FLY TYPES, OR THE SPRING FAUNA)

These are the large, dark types with black or black-and-orange bodies. They are related to the famous western salmon fly, and are tied on hooks ranging from #2, 3XL, to #8, 3XL. They imitate family Pteronarcidae, genera *Pteronarcys* and *Pteronarcella.* They are common on most salmon rivers.

The style of the fly pattern is similar to sculpin patterns, Muddlers, or Dave's Hopper, but the style is varied to simulate a stonefly more closely. These flies have a large, flat, clipped-deer-hair head, and they closely represent the classic stonefly outline. They float well and are rather durable.

HOOK:	#2–8, 3XL, Mustad streamer hook with model-perfect bend, or #1–6, TUE, RE, Mustad salmon dry-fly hook
THREAD:	black nymo or heavy monocord
TAILS:	two short fifteen-pound- to twenty-pound-test monofilament lengths dyed black, or two dark quill sections from condor or similar quill
BODY:	very dark gray or bright orange spun fur or polypropylene yarn, tied rather thick to represent the typically robust stonefly body
HACKLE:	short, very dark gray or black, tied palmer style
WINGS:	clipped section of a dark goose or turkey primary feather tied flat over the back and treated with plastic cement
LEGS AND HEAD:	dark deer hair or very dark elk hair (elk is preferable), tied Muddler style with the front part clipped flat and back fibers left long on sides to represent legs and to help float the fly
ANTENNAE:	two short ten-pound-test monofilament lengths

Pteronarcys on a salmon river

THE LARGE GOLDENS AND MEDIUM BROWNS
(THE EARLY-SUMMER FAUNA)

These flies represent the large, light-colored families, such as the brown Perlodidae family, genera *Isoperla, Isogenus,* and the yellow Perlidae family, genera *Acroneuria* and *Claassenia.*

HOOK: #4–8, 3XL, TDE, light-wire Mustad Streamer hook
TAILS: short, brown monofilament or feather fibers
BODY: tannish brown (or yellow) spun fur or polypropylene yarn
HACKLE: one short, brown feather tied palmer style
WINGS: brownish mottled turkey or similar feather section, clipped to shape and tied in flat over back, treated with plastic cement
LEGS
AND HEAD: medium deer hair clipped to sculpin-head shape, with back fibers left long on sides

Atlantic salmon big golden

Atlantic salmon small yellow

THE SMALL YELLOWS AND GREENS (THE LATE-SUMMER FAUNA)

These patterns are unusually deadly on Atlantic salmon, which seem quite often to relish greenish patterns. In green they represent the family Chloroperlidae, genus *Alloperla.* The small yellows represent the same family Chloroperlidae, but genera *Hastaperla, Swelta, Suwallia,* and six others that are yellow.

HOOK:	#8–14, 3XL, TDE, Mustad light-wire streamer hook or Mustad salmon dry-fly hook
THREAD:	fine yellow (or green) nymo or monocord
TAILS:	yellow (or green) four-pound-test monofilament or feather fibers
BODY:	bright yellow (or green) spun fur or polypropylene yarn
WINGS:	light-gray mallard primary quill section clipped to shape and tied flat over back, treated with plastic cement
LEGS AND HEAD:	light-gray or yellow (depending on genus being imitated) deer hair clipped to sculpin-head shape with back part left long on sides

Many people make the sad mistake of not trying the smaller patterns. They can be very effective when the fish are down or are hard to move. They are good in bright sunlight or when the salmon have been fished over and are wary. The small, bright greens and the tiny blacks are especially good. The very large patterns are most effective on the larger salmon in high water, fresh from the sea and not overly disturbed.

These dry stonefly patterns are at least as effective as conventional patterns, and we feel that under most conditions they are even more effective. In any case, there is no question in our minds that these drys are a joy to fish.

Wet Stonefly Patterns for Atlantic Salmon

We developed a series of squirrel-tail streamers (night flies) for large browns that are also very effective for salmon on #2 to 12, 3XL, streamer hooks. They represent a wet version of each stonefly family and are fished just under the surface or in the film with a Portland hitch. Chapter Seven, on stonefly patterns, has the exact descriptions for each family of Plecoptera, and these are designed as trout streamers.

These patterns work quite well for Atlantic salmon as tied for trout, but they can be modified a bit for a more traditional Atlantic salmon fly look with perhaps a bit of increase in effectiveness. The modifications are the addition of a tinsel tag at the end of the shank, a bright yellow or green fluorescent tip, a short double stonefly tail, and a butt of brown, black, or green ostrich fiber (color depends on the pattern). From the butt on (the body, ribbing, wing, and hackle) the pattern is exactly like the trout-fly types in Chapter Seven.

Since there are so many different stoneflies, the innovative fly tier can use his imagination and devise many new patterns that will surely be effective if the stonefly outline and color phases are represented. The green and yellow fluorescent tips add a great deal to the effectiveness of these patterns—we believe they resemble the glowing egg sac of the natural egg-laying insect. But the tier should not make the mistake of believing that if a little fluorescence is good, a lot is better. Not so. Too much destroys the whole effect. An egg-laying stonefly does not have fluorescent wings and body. These patterns are also very effective as trout flies for both night and daytime fishing, as all trout seem to relish that tiny, bright green or yellow egg sac at the end of the body.

Two examples of wet hairwing stonefly patterns for Atlantic salmon follow.

GREEN (THE SUMMER GREENS OF FAMILY CHLOROPERLIDAE, GENUS ALLOPERLA)

HOOK:	#6–12, 3XL, TDE, streamer hook
THREAD:	green monocord or nymo
TAG:	oval gold tinsel
TIP:	bright green fluorescent floss
TAIL:	two light-green feather sections or polar-bear hair
BUTT:	green or tan ostrich herl
BODY:	medium green fur
RIBBING:	oval gold tinsel
HACKLE:	yellow and green mixed, tied in as a braid
WING:	black squirrel tail and green-dyed polar bear mixed

BROWN (THE SUMMER BROWNS OF FAMILY PERLODIDAE)

HOOK:	#4–8, 3XL, TDE, streamer hook
THREAD:	brown monocord or nymo
TAG:	oval gold tinsel
TIP:	bright yellow fluorescent floss
TAIL:	two light-tan feather fibers or brown-bear hair
BUTT:	brown ostrich herl
BODY:	medium-brown spun fur
HACKLE:	tannish
WING:	fox-squirrel tail

Patterns in the correct color phases for all the separate families of Plecoptera are effective. One of the most common species of stoneflies found in Canadian trout streams and as far north as the Ungava Peninsula is *Pteronarcys doddsi.* This is the huge black of the early-spring fauna and is an eastern version of *Pteronarcys californica,* or the western salmon fly. It has a green tip, dark grayish body, and a gray squirrel-tail wing. A darkish

Muddler Minnow is a close imitation of this common species and probably explains that pattern's effectiveness for Atlantic salmon. The standard Bomber dry salmon fly also looks looks a lot like the big stoneflies and is a good pattern in all its variations.

Atlantic salmon bomber

CHAPTER SEVEN

Stonefly Patterns

IN THIS CHAPTER WE PRESENT A VARIETY OF STONEFLY PATTERNS THAT WE HAVE found to be effective imitations. We include a series of prototypical patterns, some new patterns, and some well-known stonefly imitations. The prototypical series is a small group of imitations we developed that covers about 95 percent of the stonefly species of the eight families of Plecoptera found in North American waters. They are easy to tie, and they include nymph, adult, and fluttering-adult imitations for the winter, spring, and summer stoneflies discussed in earlier chapters. Also included among the prototypical patterns is a group of squirrel-tail nymphs that we have found to be highly effective and to complement the more specific prototypical patterns. The new patterns we present include such flies as the "Heads Up" nymph and the Golden Stone Wiggle-Nymph. The traditional patterns are the effective stonefly imitations commonly in use, such as the dry Bird's Stonefly and the Sofa Pillow, both of which are popular stonefly imitations in the West.

One of our main philosophies concerning stonefly-nymph imitations is that they should be soft and resilient, like the naturals. If one squeezes a grasshopper or cricket between his thumb and forefinger, he will know the effect the fly tier should be after. Hard (and usually opaque) imitations, no matter how intricately realistic in appearance they are, will not hook many fish. They may look super, but they don't work well. We have found from experience and from observing trout in the artificial stream we constructed (described in Appendix One) that fish have an incredibly fast reaction time. They will allow the current to bring food to them, along with bits of twigs, leaves, and other material. They suck in the object and then either spit it out or swallow it, depending on the feel to the mouth. If they reject the object, it is spit out so quickly that the angler could never react in time if he noticed a pause in the line, and he certainly wouldn't *feel* the strike.

Only occasionally will a trout turn to strike a nymph with an action the angler can actually feel as a strike. It is hard to detect a take with a deeply fished nymph. If the artificial feels like a natural to the fish, it will at least hold the fly longer and may even swallow it. Flies tied in this manner will hook many more fish. In fact, many trout will hook themselves when the artificial has the same resilience as the natural.

This resilient feel can be accomplished by cutting plastic foam or foam rubber into strips and wrapping it on as an underbody. The regular body of spun fur is then wrapped over the underbody, and this produces a soft, translucent imitation that will be effective.

In Chapter Six we list some large dry-fly salmon patterns that work well for trout also, both for daytime and for night fishing. The wet salmon series mentioned in that chapter includes spruced-up versions of wet hair-wing trout flies, and they are super night flies for brown trout.

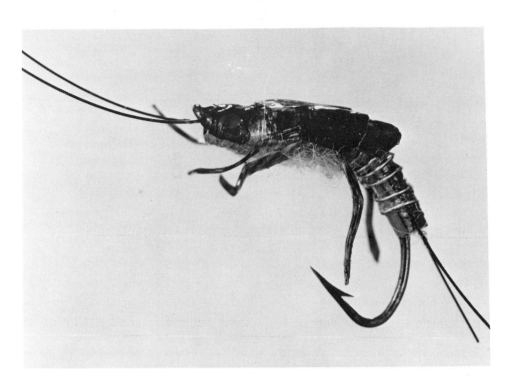

Realistic hard-body bent-hook nymph

Realistic hard-body nymph

In the section of this chapter that deals with the prototypical patterns, the reader will find both a high-riding and a low-riding type. We use each type in our dry-fly fishing. One presents a low silhouette that represents a spent or quiescent natural; the other type imitates a flying, buzzing, active natural. Both are effective at various times. Even when no large flight is present, often a few naturals can be found buzzing over the water, so these patterns are very good for searching the water. There is really no way of knowing in advance which type the fish will prefer, so the angler must try them both. Most of the float-fishing in the West is actually searching the water, and most of the time no large flight of adult naturals is present. The angler is hunting for a fish that is on the lookout for a nice meal, and both types of artificials should be tried.

When stonefly nymphs are washed away from their perch by a surge of high current, they do not swim to the safety of another rock or twig. They drift with their heads up and their six legs working frantically like pistons to grip whatever they come in contact with. A deeply fished, dead-drifted nymph is good under such circumstances. The artificial should be tied so it drifts *head up*. This can be accomplished by lightly weighting the last one-third of the hook and incorporating some foam or plastic at the head.

When the smaller greens and yellows are on the water during a warm afternoon, a simple tie consisting of a fur body with grizzly hackle tied palmer style is an exceptionally good pattern.

If the angler is tying an exact imitation for a specific species or if he is tying an alternative pattern, he shouldn't worry about being too exact with shades of color. Size and shape are far more important. Shades may even vary in individuals of the same species. That is not to say that we don't try to match the color as closely as possible. But if the angler is fishing to a selective fish with a good pattern and is not getting results, it is almost surely not the shade of the imitation that is causing the problem. It is probably something else that is responsible for the refusals from the trout.

Some interesting effects can be created for nymph imitations by bending the hook shanks either toward or away from the bend to simulate the arching or folding of the natural's body when it is dislodged and drifting in the current. Most of the nymph patterns listed in this chapter can be tied in this style if desired.

Prototypical Patterns

This series of prototypical patterns is designed to provide imitations for the more specific groups of stoneflies discussed in earlier chapters. There are nymph and adult patterns below for the winter stoneflies, the spring stoneflies (or salmon flies) and the summer stoneflies.

WINTER STONEFLIES

Tiny Winter Black Nymph (Capniidae species)

HOOK: Mustad 7957, BX, #18–16
THREAD: dark brown 6/0
TAILS: medium-brown hackle fibers
ABDOMEN: blend of ¾ medium-brown rabbit fur and ¼ yellow rabbit fur.
WING CASE: dark-brown rabbit fur spun and dubbed so that it is positioned on top of thorax or gray mallard shoulder feathers clipped to shape.
LEGS: medium-brown hackle fibers in three clumps

Tiny winter black nymph *Steve Lavely*

Tiny Winter Black Adult (Capniidae species)

HOOK:	Mustad 94840, #18–16
THREAD:	black 6/0
TAILS:	furnace or dark chocolate hackle fibers
BODY:	blend of ⅔ dark brown and ⅓ black fur or polypropylene or fur
WINGS:	furnace or coachman-brown hackle tips, tied in flat and slightly V-d out from the body or mallard duck quill segment, tied flat
HACKLE:	furnace or dark chocolate, clipped top and bottom. Leave full for high-riding pattern

Early-spring brown adult *Steve Lavely*

Early Brown Nymph (Brachyptera species)

HOOK: Mustad 7957, BX, #10–12
THREAD: dark brown 6/0
TAILS: furnace or dark-brown hackle fibers
RIB: tan thread or gold wire
ABDOMEN: chocolate brown fur
THORAX: same as abdomen
WING CASE: two black crow quill segments, clipped in V shape
LEGS: furnace or dark brown hackle fibers

Early-spring brown
nymph *Steve Lavely*

Early Brown Adult (Brachyptera species)

HOOK: Mustad 94840, #10–12
THREAD: dark brown 6/0
TAILS: furnace or dark-brown hackle fibers
BODY: chocolate-brown fur or polypropylene
WINGS: dark-brown hackle tips tied in flat and slightly V-d out from body or medium-gray mallard primary fibers
HACKLE: furnace or dark brown, clipped top and bottom. Leave full for high-riding pattern

Some wonderful wings for the dry adults can be constructed from hen hackle and body feather tips. These are tied flat and can be lacquered with some of the new nail polishes to retain their flat, naillike shape. By locating feathers from various birds, such as bobwhite, pheasant, and hen chickens, you can obtain virtually any color you may need.

SPRING STONEFLIES, OR SALMON FLIES (*Pteronarcys* and *Pteronarcella* species)

Salmon Fly Nymph

HOOK: Mustad 9672, #2–4, #8 for *Pteronarcella* and immature *Pteronarcys* species
THREAD: dark brown
TAILS: dark-brown stripped goose, tied short
RIB: tan thread or flat monofilament dyed light brown
ABDOMEN: blend of ¾ chocolate brown rabbit and ¼ orange fur (seal, seal imitation, or other translucent synthetic)
THORAX: same as abdomen, only picked out heavily on bottom
LEGS: ring-neck pheasant body feathers or mallard flank dyed dark brown

Salmon Fly Adult

HOOK: Mustad 9671, #2–4, #8 for *Pteronarcella* adult
THREAD: dark brown
TAILS: brown bucktail
BODY: orange fur or polypropylene
WINGS: brown bucktail or microweb dyed brown with a marking pen, tied in flat
HACKLE: brown, clipped top and bottom. Leave full for high-riding pattern

Salmon-fly
nymph *Steve Lavely*

Salmon-fly adult *Steve
Lavely*

Salmon Fly Fluttering Adult

HOOK: Mustad 9671, #2–4, #8 for *Pteronarcella* adult
THREAD: dark brown
TAILS: brown bucktail
RIB: palmered ginger hackle
BODY: orange floss or polypropylene, tied slim
WINGS: brown hackle tips, tied with convex sides together and slanted back at 45 degrees, or sparse brown bucktail tied at 45 degrees
HACKLE: brown

Salmon-fly fluttering
adult *Steve Lavely*

Henrys Fork Salmon Fly

HOOK:	Mustad 94831, #4
THREAD:	orange 3/0 monocord
TAIL:	black moose hair
BODY:	rusty orange dubbing palmered with a brown saddle hackle. Clip the hackle down to $1/_2$ the hook gap.
WING:	medium elk hair
HEAD:	very dark elk hair tied forward and pulled back

Trout-type improved
Henrys Fork

Improved Sofa Pillow

HOOK: Mustad 94831, #4
THREAD: orange 3/0 monocord
TAIL: black goose quill
BODY: rusty orange dubbing palmered with a furnace saddle hackle
UNDERWING: medium elk hair
OVERWING: red squirrel tail
HACKLE: two long furnace saddle hackles
HEAD: deer hair, clipped

Improved Sofa Pillow

Alloperla pacifica nymph

Isogenus decisus nymph

Acroneuria lycorias nymph

A fish's eye view of *Isogenus tostonus*—the Little Dark Olive

Four albino nymphs (Fred Oswalt)

Pheasant-wing Golden Stone

Henrys Fork Stonefly—salmon fly (Mike Lawson)

Golden Stonefly Nymph (Poul Jorgensen)

Duck-Quill Stonefly—Little Black (Mike Lawson)

Henrys Fork Salmon Fly (Mike Lawson)

Henrys Fork Golden Stone (Mike Lawson)

Lawson's Sofa Pillow—salmon fly (Mike Lawson)

Stacked Deer-Hair Stonefly (Mike Lawson)

Improved Bird's Stonefly (Mike Lawson)

Little Yellow Stonefly (Mike Lawson)

Atlantic Salmon Golden Stonefly (Dave Whitlock)

Little Yellow Stonefly for salmon (Dave Whitlock)

Streaker for salmon (Poul Jorgensen)

THE BIG GOLDENS

Big Golden Nymph (Perlidae)

HOOK: Mustad 9672, #6–8, weighted if desired, #6 needed only for *Claassenia sabulosa*

THREAD: brown 3/0 monocord

TAILS: light-brown or tan stripped goose quills, V-d and tied very short

RIB: white thread

ABDOMEN: blend of ½ light-yellow lemon rabbit fur and ½ light-brown rabbit or seal fur

THORAX: same as abdomen and picked out

WING CASE: mottled turkey quill segments or ringneck pheasant rump feathers

LEGS: brown partridge or mallard flank, dyed light brown

Big golden
nymph *Steve Lavely*

Big Golden Adult

HOOK: Mustad 94840, #6–8
THREAD: brown 3/0 monocord
TAILS: ginger hackle fibers
BODY: blend of ½ lemon yellow and ½ medium brown fur or polypropylene
WINGS: light-tan bucktail tied flat or elk hair
HACKLE: ginger

Big golden adult *Steve Lavely*

Big Golden Fluttering Adult

HOOK: Mustad 94840, #6–8
THREAD: brown 3/0 monocord
TAILS: light bucktail
RIB: light-ginger hackle, palmered
BODY: light-yellow fur or polypropylene, tied slim
WINGS: light-tan bucktail, slanted back at 45 degrees
HACKLE: ginger tied full

Big golden fluttering
adult *Steve Lavely*

SUMMER STONEFLIES—THE MEDIUM BROWNS (*Perlodidae*)

Medium Brown Nymph

HOOK: Mustad 9672, #8–14
THREAD: brown 3/0
TAILS: mallard flank, dyed brown or goose quill
RIB: pale-yellow thread or gold wire
ABDOMEN: blend of ⅔ medium-brown rabbit fur and ⅓ pale-yellow
            rabbit fur overlayed with dark mottled-brown turkey tail
            segment
THORAX: same as abdomen
WING CASE: mottled turkey quill segments
LEGS: dark-brown partridge

Fur-bodied all-purpose nymph

Medium Brown Adult

HOOK: Mustad 94840, #8–14, #8 needed for the unusually large *I. olivaceous*

THREAD: brown 3/0 monocord

TAILS: medium-brown hackle fibers or elk hair

BODY: yellowish-brown fur or polypropylene

WINGS: dark-ginger hackle tips, tied flat and slightly V-d out from the body, or medium-brown elk hair or quill segments

HACKLE: dark-ginger or medium brown, clipped top and bottom. Leave full for high-riding pattern

Little yellow/green and big golden/brown prototype

Medium Brown Fluttering Adult

HOOK: Mustad 94840, #8–14
THREAD: brown 3/0 monocord
TAILS: brown bucktail
RIB: ginger hackle palmered
BODY: tan polypropylene, tied slim
WINGS: clump of wood duck, or equivalent, tied in at 45 degrees
HACKLE: dark ginger or medium brown, tied full

Early-summer medium brown fluttering adult *Steve Lavely*

THE LITTLE GREENS AND YELLOWS (Chloroperlidae)

Little Yellow and Green Nymph:
Same as pattern used for winter stoneflies in yellow and green,
in #10, #12, #14.

Little Yellow Adult

HOOK:	Mustad 94840, #12–14
THREAD:	light olive
TAILS:	light-ginger hackle fibers
BODY:	pale-lemon yellow polypropylene
WINGS:	light-ginger hackle tips tied in flat and slightly V-d out from the body, or clump of light-ginger hackle fibers splayed over top or duck quill
HACKLE:	light ginger

Little Yellow Fluttering Adult

HOOK:	Mustad 94840, #12–14
THREAD:	light olive
TAILS:	light-ginger hackle fibers
RIB:	cream hackle, palmered
BODY:	yellow polypropylene, tied slim
UNDERWING:	wood duck or imitation, slanted back at 45 degrees
WINGS:	pair of light tannish-gray duck quill segments, slanted back, straddling the wood duck, Henryville style

Late summer yellow fluttering adult *Steve Lavely*

Little Green Adult

HOOK:	Mustad 94840, #12–14
THREAD:	olive
TAILS:	dark-ginger hackle fibers
BODY:	bright greenish fur or polypropylene
WINGS:	dark-ginger hackle tips, tied flat and slightly V-d out from the body, or a clump of dark-ginger hackle fibers splayed over top or quill segments
HACKLE:	dark ginger

Little Green Fluttering Adult

HOOK:	Mustad 94840, #12–14
THREAD:	olive
TAILS:	dark-ginger hackle fibers
RIB:	light-ginger hackle, palmered
BODY:	bright-green fur or polypropylene, tied slim
UNDERWING:	wood duck or imitation, slanted back at 45-degree angle
WINGS:	pair of gray duck quill segments, slanted back, straddling the wood duck, Henryville style

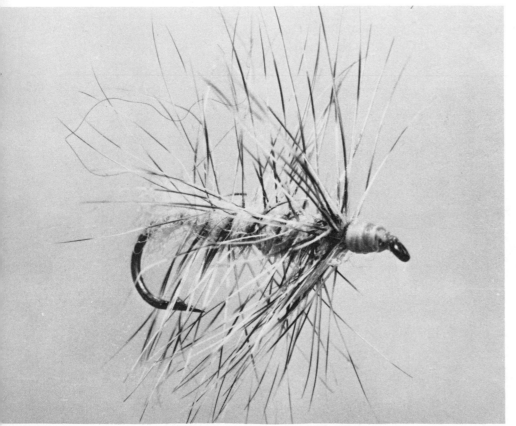

Flying green and yellow stonefly with fluorescent egg sac

Alternative Ways To Tie Stonefly Imitations

Over the years, many types of artificial patterns have evolved to imitate closely (and practically) the stoneflies found in North American waters; most of these are concerned with the larger forms, *Pteronarcys* and the Big Goldens. What follows is an extensive list of the most popular patterns— some new, others traditional. Our main objective is to convey the numerous alternatives that are available when tying stonefly imitations.

NYMPHS:

Bird's Stonefly (Gray) (for *Pteronarcys* species)

HOOK: Mustad 9672, #2–4
THREAD: yellow
TAIL: gray, stripped goose quill, tied short and V-d out
RIB: yellow thread or floss
ABDOMEN: dubbed gray muskrat or fox
THORAX: peacock herl palmered with blue-dun saddle hackle
WING CASE: ringneck pheasant quill
LEGS: none

Bird's stone gray or brown

Bird's Stone (Brown) (for *Pteronarcys* species)

HOOK: Mustad 9672, #2–4
THREAD: orange
TAIL: brown stripped goose quill, tied short and V-d out
RIB: orange thread
BODY: beaver or brown Mohlon
THORAX: peacock herl palmered with brown saddle hackle
WING CASE: turkey quill
LEGS: none

Bitch Creek (for *Pteronarcys* species)

HOOK: Mustad 9672, #2–4
THREAD: black
TAILS: white rubber strands
ABDOMEN: black chenille with a stripe of orange chenille secured by ribbing the tying thread back over the body
THORAX: black chenille palmered with brown saddle hackle
ANTENNAE: white rubber strands

Bitch Creek nymph

Golden Stone Nymph (Fred Arbona)

The merits of this pattern include its effectiveness in deceiving sophisticated trout as well as its use of an English bait hook to minimize snagging on the bottom of the stream (where it should be fished).

HOOK: Mustad 37160, #8, weighted with six inches of #2 fuse wire
THREAD: amber or yellow
TAIL: bicolor hen-pheasant fibers
RIBBING: dark-brown monocord
ABDOMEN: amber or gold sparkle yarn
THORAX: natural seal, picked out
WING CASE: mottled hen pheasant
LEGS: bicolor hen-pheasant fibers

Golden Stone (Polly Rosborough) (for Big Golden species)

HOOK: Mustad 1206, #6–8
THREAD: antique-gold belding silk
TAIL: teal, dyed gold
SHELLBACK: teal, dyed gold
RIB: antique-gold Cortecelli silk
BODY: gold Mohlon
WINGS: gold teal, $\frac{1}{3}$ the body length
LEGS: gold teal

Golden Stone Wiggle-Nymph (for Big Golden species)

Though more difficult to tie, this pattern conveys aliveness when worked through the water, and, in our opinion, is superior to the conventional single-hook imitation.

HOOK: Mustad 94840, #8 for abdomen, Mustad 7957, BX, #10 for thorax
THREAD: brown
TAILS: brown stripped goose, tied short and V-d out
RIB: brown thread or fine gold wire
ABDOMEN: blend of $\frac{1}{2}$ German fitch and $\frac{1}{2}$ light-brown rabbit fur (pale-lemon seal or lemon rabbit may be used instead of fitch)

Tails, rib and abdomen are tied to 94840 hook. Then entire bend is cut off, and the eye straightened and attached to 7957 hook Wiggle-Nymph style with fifteen-pound-test monofilament. Attach thorax, wing case and legs to 7957 hook.

THORAX: same as abdomen, heavily picked out
WING CASE: very dark brown, heavy grained rabbit fur, with lots of guardhairs, dubbed so that it is positioned on top of thorax in floating-nymph style wing case
LEGS: partridge dyed dark brown, extending out each side of thorax

Wiggle Nymph

"Heads Up" Drifting Stone (for Big Golden species)

HOOK: Mustad 9672, #6–8, rear of shank slightly weighted
THREAD: dark brown
TAILS: mallard flank dyed brown
RIB: yellow thread
ABDOMEN: brown acrylic yarn, cut up and dubbed
THORAX: dark brown polypropylene palmered with coachman or furnace saddle hackle
WING CASE: dark gray goose or crow primary quill segments

Kaufmann's Black Stone (Randall Kaufmann) (for *Pteronarcys* species)

HOOK: Mustad 1206, #6, weighted and flattened
THREAD: black
TAIL: black stripped goose quill, tied very short
RIB: black, flat monofilament
ABDOMEN: blend of 20 percent dark-brown seal, 10 percent claret seal, and 70 percent black seal
THORAX: same as abdomen
WING CASE: dyed black turkey, tied in three sections along the top of the thorax, clipped to a V shape
ANTENNAE: black stripped goose quill

"Heads-up" drifting stone nymph *Steve Lavely*

Kaufmann's Brown Salmon Stone (Randall Kaufmann) (for Pteronarcys species)

HOOK: Mustad 1206, #8, weighted and flattened
THREAD: tobacco brown
TAIL: brown stripped goose quill, tied very short
RIB: dyed dark brown, flat monofilament
ABDOMEN: blend of 30 percent reddish brown rabbit, 20 percent orange seal, and 50 percent dark brown seal. Clip off all the excess after rib is in place
THORAX: same as abdomen
WING CASE: mottled turkey, tied in three separate sections along the top of the thorax and clipped to a V shape
ANTENNAE: brown stripped goose quill

Keel Stonefly Nymph (for Big Golden species)

HOOK: Keel hook #8–10
THREAD: dark brown
TAILS: partridge or mallard flank, dyed brown
RIB: brown thread
ABDOMEN: blend of $\frac{1}{3}$ brown beaver, $\frac{1}{3}$ hare's ear, and $\frac{1}{3}$ yellow seal
THORAX: same as abdomen, heavily picked
WING CASE: dark-brown mottled turkey, divided into two segments

Keel stonefly
nymph *Steve Lavely*

Mike Lawson Salmon-fly Nymph (for *Pteronarcidae* species)

HOOK: 37160 #4–6 (#10 for *Pteronarcellas*, if needed)
THREAD: black
TAILS: black crow primary quill fibers, tied short and V-d out
ABDOMEN: black chenille
THORAX: brown chenille palmered with black saddle hackle
WING CASE: black chenille

Mike Lawson Big Golden Nymph (for Big Golden types)

HOOK: 9672 #8
THREAD: amber or yellow
TAILS: brown partridge or hen pheasant
ABDOMEN: gold Mohlon, no ribbing
THORAX: same as abdomen
WING CASE: turkey quill segment

NYMPH

Improved Montana Nymph

HOOK: Mustad 37260, #2 (curved shank) weighted
THREAD: brown 3/0 monocord
TAILS: rusty brown goose quill
BODY: black chenille
THORAX: dark-brown chenille
LEGS: black saddle hackle
WING CASE: black poly yarn pulled flat over the thorax

Nelson All-Acrylic Stonefly (Dick Nelson) (for Big Golden species)

HOOK: Mustad 9672, #2–8
THREAD: dark brown
TAILS: dark-brown acrylic yarn fibers, V-d out and cemented
RIB: yellow thread
ABDOMEN: brown acrylic yarn, combed out and reversed parallel to the shank
THORAX: brown acrylic yarn
WING CASE: dark-brown acrylic yarn, combed out, pulled over thorax and divided into two segments
LEGS: three pieces of dark-brown acrylic yarn, crossed through thorax and combed out to form six legs
ANTENNAE: dark-brown acrylic yarn fibers, V-d out and cemented

Little Red Stonefly (Ernest Schwiebert) (for Early Brown Stone, or *Brachyptera faciata*)

HOOK: Mustad 9671, #12–14
THREAD: rusty brown
TAIL: brown stripped goose quill, tied short
ABDOMEN: reddish brown floss, flattened and painted black at lateral margins, over which is wound reddish-brown flat monofilament
THORAX: same as body
WING CASE: brown mottled speckled hen
LEGS: reddish-brown hen hackle or speckled hen quill
ANTENNAE: brown stripped goose quill, tied so they flare out and away from eye of the hook

Soft, Fuzzy Black Stone (for *Pteronarcys* species)

HOOK: Mustad 9672, #2–10
THREAD: black
TAILS: dark cree hen fibers, soft and coarsely grained
ABDOMEN: Bob Jacklin's natural black dubbing. (Note: Body material is new dubbing material by Bob Jacklin. It's super for shaggy, realistic-looking nymphal bodies.)
THORAX: same as abdomen, heavily picked out
WING CASE: black crow quill segments

Soft fuzzy black stone nymph *Steve Lavely*

Soft, Fuzzy Brown Stone (for Big Golden species)

HOOK: Mustad 9672, #2–10
THREAD: dark brown
TAILS: furnace or coachman-brown hen fibers, soft and coarsely grained
ABDOMEN: Bob Jacklin's natural brown dubbing (See note at Soft, Fuzzy Black Stone)
THORAX: same as abdomen, heavily picked out
WING CASE: dark-brown turkey quill segments.

Stonefly Creeper (Art Flick) (for Big Golden species)

HOOK: Mustad 3906B, #10
THREAD: yellow
TAILS: ring-neck pheasant tail fibers
SHELLBACK: mallard dyed lemon wood duck
BODY: stripped ginger hackle stem, wrapped over with light amber seal fur, heavier for thorax
LEGS: brown partridge along sides and bottom

Ted's Stonefly (Ted Trueblood) (for *Pteronarcys* species)

HOOK: Mustad 9672, #6
THREAD: black
TAIL: black hackle fibers or gray, stripped goose quill, tied in a V shape
ABDOMEN: tobacco-brown chenille
THORAX: orange chenille palmered with a black saddle hackle
WING CASE: strands of chenille, same color as abdomen

Three-legged Salmon Fly Nymph (Ken Iwamasa)

HOOK: Mustad 9672, #6, weighted, with six inches of #2 fuse wire
THREAD: dark brown
TAILS: stripped black goose quill, tied short
SHELLBACK: black goose quill
RIB: thin monofilament, 4–5x tippet material
ABDOMEN: brownish-gray dyed seal or rabbit
THORAX: dark brownish-gray dyed seal or rabbit
WING CASE: clipped segments of goose quill sections
LEGS: 1st and 2nd legs reddish hackle, 3rd leg dark brown hackle

Three-legged Golden Stone Nymph (Ken Iwamasa)

HOOK: 3906B, #8, or equivalent, slightly bent and weighted with
            six inches of #1 fuse wire
THREAD: light yellow
TAILS: thin stripped black goose quill, or crow
SHELLBACK: light turkey quill
RIB: 6/0 yellow thread
ABDOMEN: medium-yellow seal or equivalent material
THORAX: same as abdomen
WING CASE: doubled segments of mottled turkey segments
LEGS: three separate branches of brown partridge, well marked

Vaughn's Ostrich Stone

This pattern was originated by Steve Vaughn of Burney, California. It is a unique and deadly pattern.

HOOK: Mustad 38941, #6–8
THREAD: black
TAILS: ostrich herl, six to eight strands, dark brown
ABDOMEN: ostrich herl
THORAX: ostrich herl
WING CASE: dark mottled turkey

Ostrich herl nymph

Albino Nymph (Fred Oswalt)

Most of the big goldens and the smaller, lighter-colored stoneflies have medium-brown nymphs. But just after the nymphs have shed their skins, which enables them to grow (a new instar), they look like an albino. They are a very light cream with tan ribbing and have light tan to cream wing cases. Trout seem to prefer this stage much like a bass prefers a soft rather than a hard-shelled crayfish. We can imitate the fresh instar by using any of the good nymph patterns given later, but in the colors mentioned above. This does not work with the big black stoneflies; such as *Pteronarcys* and other very dark species, because they are only slightly lighter at the new instar stage. However, the albino-nymph imitation works extremely well for the little yellows and greens, and the Big Goldens. The Red Stone Squirrel Tail is our favorite night-fishing fly, and while it doesn't look impressive, it is extremely effective. The other squirrel tails imitate the nymphs of each important stonefly family, and they should be fished when each type is expected to emerge.

CARL'S SQUIRREL-TAIL WETS SERIES

Red Stone Squirrel Tail

HOOK:	0–#6, 3XL, streamer hook
TAIL:	two red goose-quill fibers, tied in a V shape
BODY:	red wool yarn
RIB:	gold tinsel
HACKLE:	brown beard
WING:	fox-squirrel tail

Carl's favorite red stone wet

Large Black Squirrel Tail

HOOK:	#2–6, 3XL, TDE
TAIL:	two black crow fibers, tied in a V shape
BODY:	black spun fur
RIB:	silver tinsel
WING:	black squirrel tail
HACKLE:	natural black beard

Big Golden Squirrel Tail

HOOK:	#2–6, 3XL, TDE
TAIL:	light-tan fibers, tied in a V shape
BODY:	blend of yellow and light brown spun fur
RIB:	gold thread
WING:	red-squirrel or fox-squirrel tail
HACKLE:	ginger

Big Brown Squirrel Tail

HOOK:	#4–8, 3XL, TDE
TAIL:	brown feather fibers, tied in a V shape
BODY:	medium-brown spun fur
RIB:	gold tinsel
WING:	fox-squirrel tail
HACKLE:	medium brown

Small Green Squirrel Tail

HOOK:	#6–12, 3 XL, TDE
TAIL:	light-green goose fibers, tied in a V shape
BODY:	bright green spun fur
RIB:	silver tinsel
WING:	gray-squirrel tail
HACKLE:	tannish green

Small Yellow Squirrel Tail

HOOK:	#6–12
TAIL:	ginger feather fibers, tied in a V shape
BODY:	bright yellow
RIB:	gold tinsel
WING:	gray-squirrel tail
HACKLE:	ginger

This wet series can be made to look more realistic by lashing on a flat piece of shaped plastic as an underbody. The plastic can be obtained from hobby shops and cut to the desired form. It is thin and easy to manipulate. It gives the finished fly the flattish appearance of the naturals. This plastic can also be used on all the larger nymph and dry-fly patterns. The tails should be two goose or other wide, soft feather fibers from a primary or secondary flight feather, split wide and kept rather short, in the manner of the natural. The hairwing should extend just beyond the bend of the hook. The ribs can be flat nylon or Swannundaze dyed yellow or dark brown as an alternative to gold or silver tinsel to produce a more exact imitation. A small tip of flourescent yellow or green to imitate an egg sac often increases the effectiveness of the pattern by as much as 50 percent. The heads should be large and flattish, which shape is formed by the forward part of the tapered plastic underbody. The hackle is tied in beard or DeFeo style. If we want a weighted version we lash lead wire to either side of the hook shank instead of using the plastic underbody. These weighted flies fished in the deepest runs are deadly at night.

DRY PATTERNS

Carl's Favorite Dry Stonefly Pattern

This is one of Carl's favorite imitations for medium and small stoneflies; it is easy to tie and quite realistic in appearance. It complements the specific prototypical patterns given in Chapter Seven. It can be used as an imitation for any family when tied in the appropriate size and color. It can also be used as a general type to imitate any species, using exact shades of colors for any species the angler may find common on his favorite waters.

HOOK: #8–16, 3x fine wire TDE.
TAILS: two fibers from a primary duck wing, tied short and spread wide
BODY: spun fur of appropriate shade, tied on 2/3 of the shank from bend to hook eye to leave plenty of room for hackle and wings
HACKLE: one top-quality cock hackle, clipped off top of hook shank after being wound to leave room for wing
WING: two hen hackle or hen body feathers of appropriate color for species of stonefly being imitated; these are moistened with a good-quality nail polish or vinyl cement and tied flat over the body after the hackle has been wound and clipped on top

Later, when on the stream, if the fisherman needs a pattern that lies flush on the surface, he may clip the hackle fibers off the bottom.

The next three patterns are reverse hackle-wing dry flies by Andy Carlson of Victor, Montana. Andy is a very knowledgeable angler and is an expert on Plecoptera.

Bitterroot Stonefly (Imitates the common golden stonefly, an *Acroneuria*)

HOOK:	Mustad 94840, #8
THREAD:	salmon orange or yellow, $\frac{3}{0}$
ABDOMEN:	golden-yellow Fly-Rite dubbing or an off-yellow color
THORAX:	salmon orange
WING:	two slate reversed web hackle wings; very long-fibered Chinese hackle works best
PALMERED HACKLE:	blue dun over abdomen and thorax
HACKLE:	brown, dry-fly style

Early Stonefly (*Capnia*)

HOOK:	Mustad 94840, #16–18
THREAD:	gray $\frac{3}{0}$, $\frac{6}{0}$ on smaller hook sizes
ABDOMEN:	medium-gray to black dubbing
THORAX:	same as abdomen
WING:	slate reversed web hackle wings
HACKLE:	blue dun, dry-fly style
PALMERED HACKLE:	optional; if applied it should match the body color

Little Green Stonefly (*Chloroperla coloradensis*)

HOOK:	Mustad 94840, #14–16
THREAD:	olive $\frac{3}{0}$
ABDOMEN:	lime-green dubbing
THORAX:	same as abdomen
WING:	medium olive, reverse web hackle wing
HACKLE:	medium olive, dry-fly style
PALMERED HACKLE:	thorax only, blue dun

Drowning Stone

This is a simple pattern, for use as a wet fly, and one of the most deadly we have used.

TAILS:	short, soft-brown hen hackle fibers
BODY:	chocolate brown fur
WINGS:	tan or brown hen-hackle tips, tied similar to wings on Hen Spinner, only angled back at 45 degrees

Extended-Body Stonefly (Mike Lawson)

HOOK: Mustad 94840, #8–10; use a hook several sizes smaller than fly being tied
THREAD: dark brown
BODY: clump of deer body hair, extending shank length beyond the bend of the hook, ribbed crisscross style with tying thread
WING: deer body hair or brown bucktail, splayed over the body
HACKLE: brown

Drowning stone   *Steve Lavely*

Extended-body stone
Steve Lavely

Golden Stone

HOOK: Mustad 94840, #8–10
THREAD: yellow
RIB: light-ginger hackle, palmered and clipped
BODY: golden yellow yarn
WING: light elk hair, splayed back
HACKLE: light ginger

Microweb Stonefly (Hank Leonhard and Bill Luzardo)

HOOK: Mustad 94840, size depends upon the type of stonefly being imitated
THREAD: brown
TAILS: brown bucktail
BODY: tannish brown fur or polypropylene
WINGS: Microweb wing material, tinted brown with Pantone marking pen and cut to shape
HACKLE: coachman or dark brown

Parks' Salmon Fly (Merton Parks)

HOOK: Mustad 9671, #4–6
THREAD: black monocord, size A
TAIL: brown bucktail
RIB: brown hackle, palmered and trimmed
BODY: tangerine-orange yarn
WING: brown bucktail
HACKLE: dark brown saddle hackle

Stephenson's Fluttering Stone

HOOK: Mustad 94840, #4–6
THREAD: orange monocord, size A
TAIL: orange polypropylene yarn, knotted to reduce fraying
WING: deer body hair, long and tied in at tail position
BODY: densely palmered furnace saddle
HACKLE: same as body
ANTENNAE: stripped brown hackle stems

Bird's Stonefly

This is one of the best adult patterns, it floats low and is very realistic

HOOK: Mustad 9671, #4–6
THREAD: yellow
TAIL: brown hackle stems or monofilament dyed brown
RIB: brown hackle, palmered and trimmed
BODY: yellow floss
WING: light-brown bucktail
HACKLE: brown saddle hackle, trimmed top and bottom

Bird's Stone

Bird's Stone regular

Studying and Collecting

How to get started as an amateur entomologist

You have decided that the study of aquatic entomology might be interesting—as well as helpful in hooking more fish. Very well, how do you begin? First you will need some basic equipment and reference works. The most important tool you should acquire is a wide-field, low-power microscope. You can spend a small fortune for one if you wish, but it is not necessary. An Olympus or Nikon is impres-

Some simple, inexpensive microscopes, collecting bottles, and instruments

sive and fun to work with, but a serviceable piece of equipment (such as a Bushnell) can be purchased for much less. Your local camera, medical, or dental supply shop, high school or college biological department will have information on all types. A good source of equipment for beginners is a hobby shop. It will usually have in stock chemical and biology kits for young students at a nominal cost. Occasionally a high-power microscope is needed and the hobby shop is an ideal place to acquire one. Add a few collecting bottles, tweezers, teasing needles, scalpels, scissors, and you are in business.

Once you have the equipment, you need the reference books. These you can borrow from general libraries or, better yet, a college library. They can also be bought from the Entomological Reprint Specialists. Write to them at P.O. Box 77224, Dockweiler Station, Los Angeles, California 90007 or call them at (213) 227-1285 and they will send you a complete list of works available.

The most useful books for stoneflies are *The Stone Flies (Plecoptera) of the Rocky Mountains* by R. W. Baumann, A. R. Gaufin, and R. F. Surdick, and *Plecoptera or Stone Flies of Connecticut* by S. W. Hitchcock. We suggest you start with stoneflies since they are much less complicated for the beginner. Mayflies are next and caddis are a real challenge. It took us about forty-five minutes to key out our first stonefly to the species level and eight hours for our first caddis. A little professional help is a real time saver and can usually be obtained from a close-by college or university zoology department. These people are almost always willing to help with equipment, books, and knowledge.

If you are most interested in mayflies, which was our first study, three "must"

Some basic
entomological books
and tools *J. Frederic
Oswalt*

books are *The Mayflies of North and Central America* by George F. Edmunds, Jr., Steven L. Jenson, and Lewis Berner. This is the last word on Ephemeroptera and every serious fly fisherman should have a copy. *Mayflies of Michigan Trout Streams* by Justin W. Leonard and Fannie A. Leonard is a much easier work to master. Although it is somewhat out of date, it is a good one to start with. *The Biology of Mayflies* by Needham, Traver, and Hsu is the original "bible" of Ephemeroptera.

If your main interest is caddisflies, God help you! It is not a place for beginners. They are the toughest of the lot, but a good book to help you get started is *The Caddis Flies, or Trichoptera, of Illinois,* by Ross, as well as *Larvae of the North American Caddisfly Genera (Trichoptera)* by Glenn Wiggins.

A good, up-to-date general work on all aquatic insects is *An Introduction to Aquatic Insects of North America* edited by R. W. Merritt and K. W. Cummins. It is a broad view of all aquatic insects and is a good place to begin your study, no matter which particular insect order you are especially interested in.

After you get the equipment and the books, it is necessary to learn to use the keys in the books to identify an insect as to order, family, genus, and species. All the books have keys and line drawings to help you work your way through. Collect your specimens from a local river or lake, transfer them home, place them in a home aquarium, or preserve them for later study. Once you have a specimen to study (either a nymph or adult) you can slug it out yourself as we did at first, or you can get some expert assistance. A little help will save you much time; if you can get it, do so. Whichever route you take, it is a fascinating study and will surely help you in many ways, not the least of which is more hooked fish.

A river in your basement

The study of trout-stream insects can, of course, be kept very simple if that is one's desire. If the angler can differentiate between the major insect orders—stoneflies, caddisflies, mayflies, and midges—and acquire the ability to pick an appropriate pattern for each, he can be a successful fish catcher. On the other hand, the study can become elaborate and time consuming if one wished to obtain the knowledge and ability to identify insects to the species level. This knowledge will seem to many to be gilding the lily, but it will enhance the angler's ability to raise trout, because each species has slightly different habits and the skill to match these habits and to choose the exact fly pattern to do it with will catch the fly fisherman more fish. To some people the entomological aspect will become more important than the fish-catching. The once-small group of angler-entomologists is now a fast-growing group of enthusiasts. If an angler is, or wishes to become one of this group, he need not nor is it desirable to confine the study to streamside experience alone. This greatly restricts the scope of the study and the time available for it.

It is easily possible to bring the stream into the comfort and convenience of the home study, workshop, or laboratory. It is possible and desirable to conduct this study at a leisurely, continuing pace. It is entirely possible to create a running river in one's basement where he can study it intensely or look in on it casually ev-

A home aquarium with a
six-mile-an-hour current

eryday. With the apparatus we will describe, one can create a complete river with fast currents, riffles, pools, and even waterfalls in one's home, and it is relatively inexpensive. This river can be made elaborate, with many segments, or simple, with as few as one or two segments. It can reconstruct the entire ecosystem of a trout stream in miniature, including plants, aquatic insects, and even small fish.

Periodic trips to trout streams can be made to collect specimens. Insects, minnows, sculpins, crayfish, plants, and young-of-the-year trout can all be easily captured in seines or drift nets and transported to the home in insulated coolers. These specimens can be separated, left together, or inserted in various segments of the basement river in any mix desired. Some sections may contain fish life, others may not.

An infinite number of experiments can be carried out simultaneously, not only during the summer months but all during the often dull, frigid winter. This allows the angler to experience a completely new dimension in the study of aquatic insects and trout as they feed and live and grow together. To be able to watch and study all these things taking place *from an underwater aspect* (seeing through the glass sides of the river) gives the angler an insight to and a unique perspective on a trout-stream environment, an insight and perspective that otherwise would be difficult if not impossible to achieve. New discoveries are almost inevitable, and the advantages to the observant fly tier are endless. Not only will the fly tier benefit, but he will find with this set up he will get good hatches, and the entire emergence process can be studied, and the insects copied. Rocks and twigs can be provided in isolated sections of the miniature river for stonefly nymphs to crawl out on in their emergence process. In other sections mayfly nymphs and caddisfly larvae may be studied.

In short, one of the most useful tools an angler-entomologist can possibly have to facilitate the study of his most fascinating of sports is an artificial river in his basement. We developed this idea because certain insect species, some mayflies but particularly stonefly nymphs, require rather fast water with abundant oxygen. Others need slow or silty flows. We believed if we could set up a miniature river in the basement, where it is generally cool even in the dog days of August, we could see exactly how these stonefly nymphs and immature forms of other insect orders behave as they are growing, shedding their skins, feeding, and emerging.

Briefly, our simplest river consists of a long saltwater aquarium (at least six feet long), a high-volume water pump, two air pumps with large air stones and an under-gravel filter system. All these materials can be purchased at any good pet shop that carries saltwater fish. Our first set-up was a six-foot seventy-gallon saltwater aquarium with a Diatom filter reworked (new motor bearings and water pick-up system) to convert it to a 300-gallon-per-hour, self-contained water pump. By the time the reader reads this his local pet store will probably be able to provide even better, less expensive equipment for this purpose. Fluorescent lighting provides necessary light.

The long aquarium can quite often be purchased from the pet shop at their cost. They sell these large aquariums at cost in order to acquire new customers for their very expensive saltwater fish and other paraphernalia.

An under-the-gravel filter system is placed in the bottom of the aquarium and then three or four inches of streambed gravel is placed over the top of it.

The high-volume water pump is hooked up as illustrated so that the water is drawn from the bottom of the aquarium, from underneath the filter through the gravel down to the pump and then forced across the top of the aquarium at a rather high current speed.

The two air pumps (we use Whisper 800 models) are hooked up to two long (six-inch) air stones that are then placed at either end of the tank for extra airation. The bacteria that will become established in the gravel will filter and clean the water so that it will always remain clear and pure. The current across the top simulates a current in a river and the large air stones oxygenate the water extremely well, well enough for almost any kind of aquatic insect that is used to fast, cold rivers. Usually, if the aquarium is kept in the basement it will be cool enough—70 degrees or less. If it is impossible to place it in such a location, a water cooler (such as the type used in business offices) can be modified to provide the colder water necessary for trout and trout-stream insects.

Another more elaborate method of creating an artifical stream that would be considerably less expensive and that would give the effect of pools and falls, would be three or more small aquariums (five- to ten-gallon capacity) arranged on a shelf or table so each is lower than the preceeding one, as shown in the diagram. A high-speed water pump evacuates water from the lower tank and the water is recirculated to the highest tank. An overflow tube leads to the next lowest tank until the water returns to the water pump, and the whole process is continued. The water dropping from the top tank to the lower tanks creates a current and also airates the water. One could create an elaborate set-up by using one large saltwater set-up and connecting it to a series of three to ten or more smaller tanks in almost any combination so the artificial stream is around the entire room using all four walls. An elaborate set-up such as this is certainly not necessary but would be extremely interesting to construct and study. Many experiments could be conducted simultaneously with such an apparatus.

Last summer, by accident, we caught a couple of fingerling brown trout in the seining net while we were collecting stonefly nymphs. These were dumped into the aquarium along with everything else and were not noticed for a couple of weeks. They started growing and provided such interesting observations that we left them in the aquarium. Tremendous amounts of data about trout habits can be gleaned by watching a fingerling grow to a ten-inch fish.

One rather startling thing that we learned about trout is that as they hover in the current watching for food, the current will bring bits and pieces of bark and leaves to the fish and also small nymphs. Most of the time the trout will allow the current to bring a little piece of flotsam into its mouth, taste it, and spit it out so fast—in a microsecond it seems—that no angler could possibly feel the strike let alone have time to strike back if it were an artificial fly. Only once in about twenty times does a trout actually turn in such a way when he takes that an angler would feel the strike. This led us to the idea of having the artificial nymph feel to the trout's mouth as the natural nymph feels. In other words, a resilient artificial. (It probably explains the greater effectiveness of soft fur nymphs over hard ones.) This is especially important in large stonefly imitations, which have not proved in the past to be very effective. Eventually, of course, we had to remove the fish as they became large enough to eat the nymphs we were studying. If we had the more elaborate, compartmentalized setup at the time we could have kept the stoneflies and the fish and studied both simultaneously.

Collecting and preserving

Collecting adult stoneflies is often quite easy. Many species can be found on bushes and alders beside the river. Sometimes many stonefly adults can be collected by shaking small trees. Some species are attracted to lights at night, and others can be found in the grasses near rivers. During the egg-laying flights a butterfly net is often extremely useful. The nymphs of the stonefly are sometimes found by lifting fairly large stones from the riffles and the pools just below the riffles. Many stonefly nymphs will cling to rocks, and simply picking the rocks up and turning them over will uncover many species.

A long-handled seine with a fine mesh is useful for capturing nymphs in the deep riffles. One must place the net downstream from his position and dislodge rocks with his feet. The nymphs, carried by the current, will drift into the net.

Catching stonefly adults *J. Frederic Oswalt*

Captured nymphs can be kept alive in the field by keeping them in a styrofoam cooler or a floating rearing cage. The insects then can be transported home in large coolers with ice to slow their need for oxygen. We have kept them alive for three days in this manner.

Specimens can be preserved in simple rubbing alcohol. It should be replaced after a few days when it darkens. There are many more sophisticated mediums in use by professional entomologists, but they are more complicated. George Edmunds recommends 80 percent ethyl alcohol with 1 percent Ionol (an antioxidant) added. The Ionol lessens the bleaching. A. W. Provonsha states that specimens keep their color if heated in water to almost boiling for a few minutes. Modified Carnoy fluid and Kahles fluid are more complicated formulas used by professionals, but for an angler's purposes, too complicated for all but the most serious angler-entomologist. Adults can be pinned, and they keep their color better in this

Placing a two-pole net to capture stonefly nymphs
J. Frederic Oswalt

Picking stonefly
nymphs from the
meshes of the net
J. Frederic Oswalt

manner than any fluid allows, and they last longer if it is properly done. They
should be kept in a dark, dust-free container with a tight lid.

Specimens should always be labeled. Rag-bond paper is best. The information
should include the collecting site, date, and collector's name. Other information,
such as water type, can be added.

The equipment we used for our study of stoneflies included a wide-field, low-
power dissecting microscope, teasing needles, soft tweezers, small, eye-surgery
scalpel, 3-dram viles with labels and stoppers, and such reference books as *Stone
Flies of The Rocky Mountains* and *Stone Flies of Connecticut.*

Taxonomic Keys to
Stoneflies of Importance to Anglers

This section is not for everyone. There are those who will not want to go this far into aquatic entomology. Most fly fishermen probably wish to know just enough about insects to recognize them and the stage of their emergence or spinner fall in order to maximize their success astream. It is for the growing group of enthusiasts and amateur entomologists—that we have included this appendix.

This appendix should be considered an overview of the order Plecoptera, an *introduction* to the methods of determining the family, genus, and species of an insect the reader is interested in. We must reemphasize this is merely an introduction to the methods that determine the scientific classification of stoneflies. A full treatment and determination to the species level would take up a whole book in itself.

In this appendix we list the eight families of stoneflies, and by a series of keys explain how one can determine to which family a particular insect he is examining belongs. A similar set of keys can be used to determine the genus and species. Due to limited space these latter keys cannot be included. We recommend these two books in particular for those who wish to pursue the study. If the reader desires to learn to identify Plecoptera to the genus or species level, he should have *The Stoneflies (Plecoptera) of the Rocky Mountains* by Richard W. Baumann, Arden R. Gaufin, and Rebecca F. Surdick, published by the American Entomological Society at the Academy of Natural Sciences, Philadelphia, 1977, and *Plecoptera or Stoneflies of Connecticut* by Stephen W. Hitchcock, State Geological and Natural History Survey of Connecticut, 1974. These are scientific works by entomologists. The latter is mainly about the East and the former concerns the West, and both are current. The eastern work uses a modified classification of Ricker (1952). It is the simplest and the classification we use in the previous chapters of this book. The volume on western stoneflies uses a classification based on Zwick (1969), which is more exacting. In it certain subgenus classifications are raised to distinct groups or full genus level, causing many species to be put into a new genera. For example, under the old classification the early brown stonefly of the East is family Taeniopterygidae, genus *Brachyptera*, species *fasciata*. Under the new classification the genus is rechanged to *Strophopteryx*, and everything else is the same.

In order to learn the methods of classifying insects it is necessary to understand how all living things are grouped. All living things are either plant or animal. All members of the plant and animal kingdom are classified under categories that represent relationships to each other. Here is an example:

> Kingdom: animal (all animal life)
> Subkingdom: invertebrate (all animals without backbones)
> Phylum: arthropoda (all animals with external skeletons, bilateral symmetry, jointed legs)
> Class: insecta (all true insects)
> Order: Plecoptera (stoneflies)
> Family: Pteronarcidae
> Genus: *Pteronarcys*
> Species: *californica*

The following are keys to the families of stoneflies. These keys will allow the reader to discover to which large group or family a particular stonefly belongs. If one desires to delve further into stoneflies, he should obtain the two books previously mentioned for the keys to the genera and species. This key is from *The Stoneflies (Plecoptera) of the Rocky Mountains*, which we have adapted to the angler's needs.

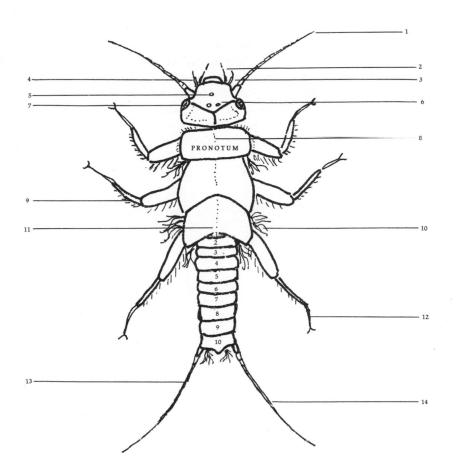

PRONOTUM

1. ANTENNA

2. MAXILLARY PALPS

3. LABIAL PALPS

4. LABRUM

5. MEDIAN OCELLUS

6. LATERAL OCELLUS

7. COMPOUND EYE

8. DORSAL SITURE

9. HAIR FRINGE

10. THORACIC GILL

11. WING PAD

12. TARSUS

    A) FIRST SEGMENT

    B) SECOND SEGMENT

    C) THIRD SEGMENT

13. ANAL GILL

14. CERCUS

Key to the Families

MALES AND FEMALES

1. Paraglossae and glossae of about equal length (fig. 1) 2
   Paraglossae much longer than glossae (fig. 2) 7
2. Anterior abdominal sterna with branched gill remnants (fig. 3); anal area of
   forewings with two or more full rows of crossveins (fig. 4) .....Pteronarcidae
   Abdominal sterna without branched gill remnants; anal area of forewings
   without crossveins or with only one row 3
3. Ocelli two; form roachlike (fig. 5); ten or more costal crossveins in forewings
   ....Peltoperlidae

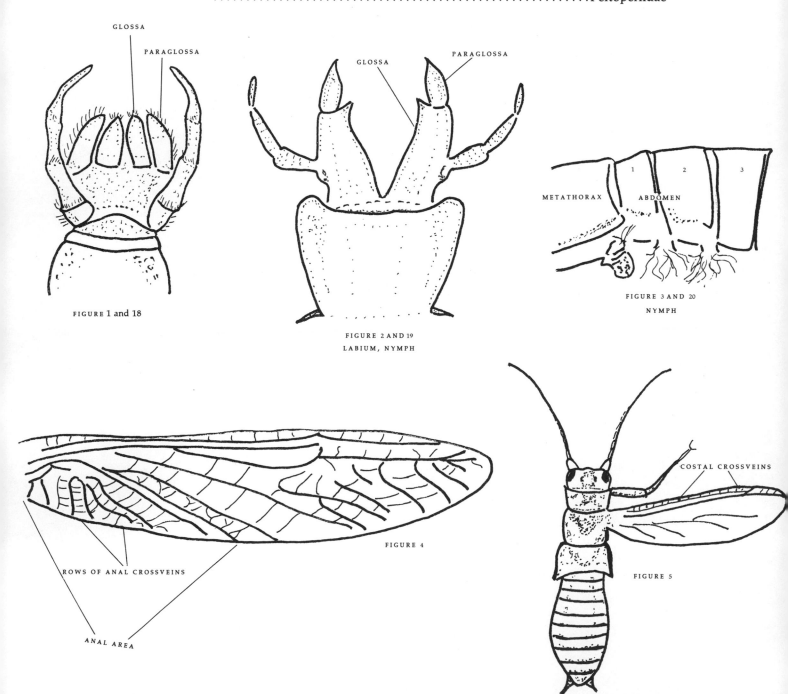

GLOSSA
PARAGLOSSA

FIGURE 1 and 18

GLOSSA   PARAGLOSSA

FIGURE 2 AND 19
LABIUM, NYMPH

METATHORAX   ABDOMEN

FIGURE 3 AND 20
NYMPH

ROWS OF ANAL CROSSVEINS

ANAL AREA

FIGURE 4

COSTAL CROSSVEINS

FIGURE 5

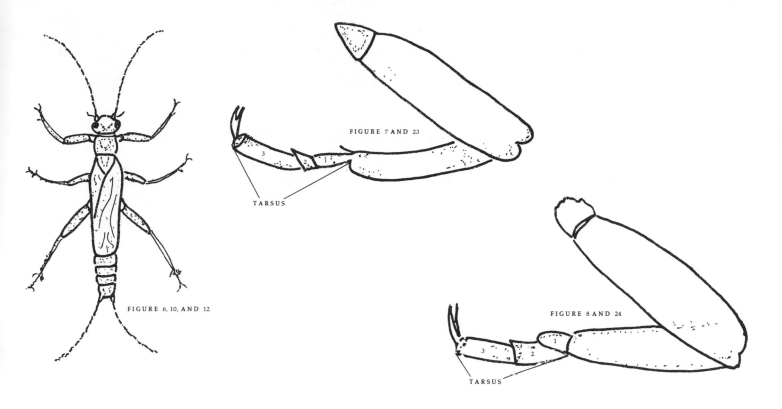

FIGURE 7 AND 23

TARSUS

FIGURE 6, 10, AND 12

FIGURE 8 AND 24

TARSUS

Ocelli three; form elongate (fig. 6); less than ten costal crossveins in forewings, except in *Isocapnia,* which may have ten or more 4
4. Second tarsal segment much shorter than first (fig. 7) 5
Second tarsal segment at least as long as first (fig. 8) . . . . Taeniopterygidae
5. General form stout and rather robust; X-shaped pattern present in forewings at cord (fig. 9) . . . . Nemouridae
General form thin and elongate (fig. 10), except *Megaleuctra,* which is quite stout; X-shaped pattern absent from forewings at cord (fig. 11) 6

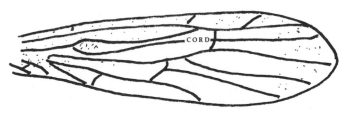

FIGURE 11

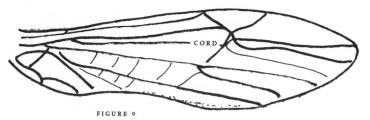

FIGURE 9

6. Wings lying flat at rest; cerci with four or more segments (fig. 12 and fig. 13) . . . . .Capniidae
   Wings slightly rolled when at rest; cerci one segmented (fig. 14 and fig. 15) . . . . .Leuctridae
7. Branched gill remnants present at lower angles of thorax . . . . .Perlidae
   Branched gill remnants absent from lower angles of thorax 8

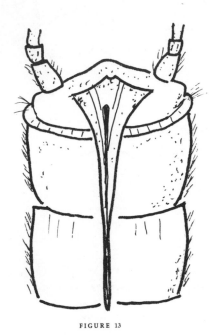

FIGURE 13

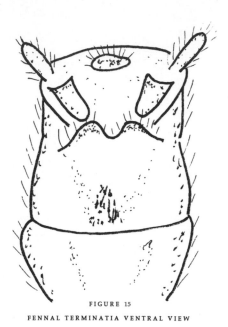

FIGURE 15

FENNAL TERMINATIA VENTRAL VIEW

8. External gill remnants entirely lacking; second anal vein of forewing not forked or forked beyond anal cell, except in *Kathroperla,* which has the fork at margin of cell or included in it (fig. 16) . . . . .Chloroperlidae
   External gill remnants simple or absent; fork of second anal vein of forewing included in anal cell, so that its branches leave cell separately (fig. 17) Perlodidae

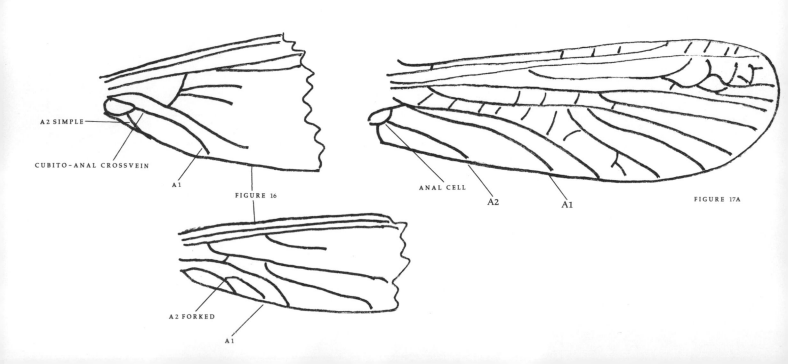

A2 SIMPLE

CUBITO-ANAL CROSSVEIN

A1

FIGURE 16

ANAL CELL

A2

A1

FIGURE 17A

A2 FORKED

A1

MATURE NYMPHS

1. Paraglossae and glossae of equal length (fig. 18) 2
   Paraglossae much longer than glossae (fig. 19) 7
2. Anterior abdominal sterna with branched gills (fig. 20) . . . . Pteronarcidae
   Abdominal sterna without branched gills 3
3. Ocelli two; form roachlike (fig. 21); thoracic sterna overlapping next segment
   . . . . Peltoperlidae
   Ocelli three; form elongate (fig. 22); thoracic sterna not overlapping next seg-
   ment 4
4. Second tarsal segment much shorter than first (fig. 23) 5
   Second tarsal segment at least as long as first (fig. 24) . . . . . . Taeniopterygidae
5. Form stout with hindwing pads strongly divergent from body axis (fig. 25) Nemouridae
   Form elongate and cylindrical with hindwing pads nearly parallel (fig. 26) . . 6

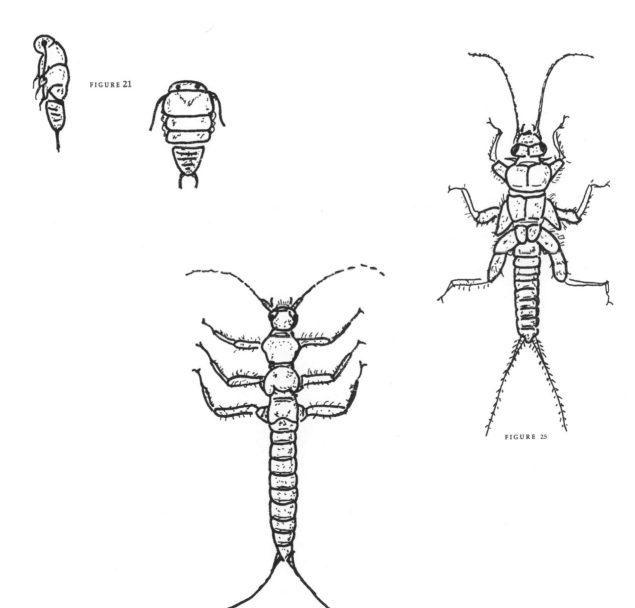

FIGURE 21

FIGURE 25

FIGURE 32

6. Notch on inner margins of hindwing pads located on anterior third; abdominal segments one to nine divided by a membranous fold laterally (fig. 27) Capniidae

Notch on inner margins of hindwing pad located on posterior third; at most only the first seven abdominal segments divided by a membranous fold (fig. 28) ....Leuctridae

FIGURE 27

FIGURE 28

7. Branched gills present at lower angles of thorax; apex of glossae rounded Perlidae

Branched gills absent from thorax; apex of glossae pointed 8

8. Dorsal surface usually pigmented in distinct pattern; cerci as long as or longer than abdomen; hindwing pads of mature nymphs diverging from body axis (fig. 29 and fig. 30) ....Perlodidae

Dorsal surface concolorous; cerci not more than three fourths as long as abdo-

FIGURE 29

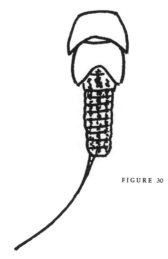

FIGURE 30

men; hindwing pads nearly parallel to body axis, except in *Kathroperla,* which has an elongate head (fig. 31 and fig. 32) .Chloroperlidae

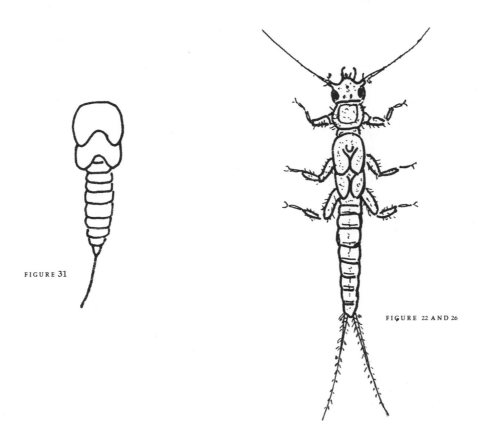

FIGURE 31

FIGURE 22 AND 26

This chapter is meant to be an *orientation* to the order for the amateur student of Plecoptera, a general introduction, a place to start. Many of the genera of the same family are similar and most of the species within that genera are almost identical. Strictly from a fisherman's point of view, it is enough to be able to identify the family and know it's a big black salmon fly or a small green or a big golden. For those who wish to delve more deeply, the following should be helpful as a start.

The following is a list of the most modern classification of stoneflies with all the genera, number of species in that genera, and some of the most common species that we as trout fishermen are interested in:

PNA—Pan-North America   ENA—East
ANA—Amphi-North America
NNA—Northern North America   WNA—Western North America

The Mottled Browns of Summer

FAMILY NEMOURIDAE

These are the most common stoneflies in most of the Rockies. Nymphs are small and stout bodied with numerous hairs and spines on the dorsal surface and appendages. Adults are easily recognized by the distinctive X on the forewing at the cord. They are often the dominant primary consumers in the flowing water ecosystems, are detrivores, and act as shredders of materials, such as leaves, that enter the river from the outside. They range in size from 6–10mm.

1) Genus *Amphinemura.* Not common in Rockies, except in some southern locales, except *A. linda,* which is found further north. Nymphs require clean cold water of permanent streams. Six species:
   a. *banski.* Common; emerges July–August Rocky Mountain National Park.
   b. *linda.* Common in Alaska, Canada, and midwestern U.S.; emerges June–August.
   c. *mogollonica.* Common in southern Rocky Mountains; emerges July–August.
   d. *nigrita.* East
   e. *apache.* West
   f. *mogollonica.* southern Midwest.

2) Genus *Malenka.* Eleven species; common in WNA and PNA; adults are small and brown and frail; most common genus in large and small springs in West; emerges late summer and early fall.
   a. *californica.* Common in small creeks and rivers in fall.
   b. *coloradensis.* Widely distributed in southern Rocky Mountains; emerges June–November.
   c. *flexura.* Common in spring in creeks and small rivers; emerges March–December.

3) Genus *Lednia.* One species WNA; uncommon.
   a. *tumana.* Found only in Glacier National Park.

4) Genus *Nemoura.* Four species NNA extent; common in Europe and Asia, but only in northern locales in North America; circumpolar.
   a. *artica.* emerges June–August; WNA.
   b. *trispinosa.* ENA.

5) Genus *Podmosta.* Small creeks at high elevations; they are small in size and uncommon; WNA.
   a. *delicatula.* Most common species.

6) Genus *Paranemoura.* One species; ENA.
   a. *perfecta.* Northeast; found in small brooks in New England.

7) Genus *Ostrocerce.* One species; ANA.
   a. Uncommon species.

8) Genus *Frostoia.* Three species ANA; can be abundant in lowlands, creeks, and rivers: flush in early spring; adults are small and move quickly.

a. *besametsa.* Common in all creeks and rivers; emerges March–August.
b. *completa.* East; 6–8mm.
c. *simulus.* Uncommon.

9) Genus *Soyedina.* Seven species; found in small creeks and seeps, sometimes no running water; ENA; WNA.
    a. *potteri.* Only species in Rocky Mountains; emerges April–July; uncommon.
    b. *interupta.* Cascade Mountains; Pacific Northwest.
    c. *producta.* Cascade Mountains.
    d. *valicularia.* ENA; 10–12mm.

10) Genus *Visoka.* One species; WNA.
    a. *cataractae.* Very rapid creeks; emerges March–July.

11) Genus *Zapada.* Most common genus of the family; species are found in every flowing-water ecosystem in the northern Rocky Mountains. *A. cinctipes* is the widest ranging species of the whole group. Abundant in accumulations of leaf materials and act as shredders. Eight species.
    a. *cinctipes.* All Rocky Mountain systems excluding Arizona; most common; emerges February–August; everywhere; twelve months; emerges from spring-fed systems.
    b. *cordillera.* Uncommon.
    c. *glacier.* Uncommon.
    d. *haysi.* Widely distributed, but not common. emerges April–July.
    e. *oregonensis.* Pacific Northwest.
    f. *columbina.* Northern Rocky Mountains.

The Spring Blacks and Browns

FAMILY TAENIOPTERYGIDAE

These are very similar to family Nemouridae. Nymphs are stout and wing pads are divergent from the body axis. Adults are brown or black, medium to medium large, and after emerging fly to nearby vegetation. A spring emerger except at very high altitudes, where they emerge later.

1) Genus *Bolotoperla.* One species ENA.
    a. *rossi.* 15–20mm.

2) Genus *Doddsia.* WNA; high elevations in creeks and small rivers.
    a. *occidentalis.* WNA; emerges February–May; 15–20mm.

3) Genus *Oemopteryx.* Found in large, silty, but unpolluted rivers. Males have short thin forewings, bent abruptly upward near apex and are flightless. Missouri, Colorado and Saskatchewan river systems. Four species.
    a. *fosketti.* Western; found in large rivers.

b. *galacillis.* Common in East; other two species uncommon.

4) Genus *Taenionema.* One species eastern, seven species western. Species produce flush hatches.

    a. *nigripenne.* WNA very common, Adults have light and dark color phases, Emerges March–August.

    b. *pacificum.* Mostly in rivers in the North. Emerges March–July.

    c. *pallidum.* Western United States, Canada.

    d. *atlantica.* Eastern.

5) Genus *Strophopteryx.* Seven species. ENA.

    a. *fasciata.* Flick's #14 Little Early Brown. Other species regional, uncommon.

6) Genus *Taeniopteryx.* Nine species, very common in eastern and midwestern North America. Early spring emergences, rare in West. Lives in bank vegetation of permanent streams. One-year life cycle.

    a. *nivalis.* Most abundant of eastern winter stoneflies. Rogue (Michigan). Little Black of the Rogue.

    b. *paruvla*

    c. *borski.* Most common.

Tiny Winter Blacks

FAMILY CAPNIIDAE

1) Genus *Allocapnia.* Thirty-eight species eastern and midwestern America, 4–10mm.

    a. *allocapnia*

    b. *illinoensis*

    c. *minima*

    d. *nivicola*

    e. *pygmaea*

    f. *forbesi*

    g. *mystica*

    h. *recta*

    i. *rickeri.* Important and common.

    j. *vivipara*

2) Genus *Bolschecapnia.* Four species WNA. Larger than other genera. Emerges early spring in lower elevations but later in higher elevations.

    a. *gregsoni.* Uncommon, April–July, only at lakes in very high elevations, Canadian Rockies.

    b. *milami.* Canadian and Northern Rockies. Uncommon. Emerges March.

    c. *sasquatchi.* Cascade and Rocky Mountains, northern. Emerges March. Uncommon.

    d. *spenceri.* Canadian and northern Rockies. Emerges June–August, creeks and rivers, but one of the few to occur in lakes. Abundant in Iceberg Glacier National Park.

3) Genus *Capnia.* 4–10mm. Small black species, fifty species WNA, NNA. When studied, more will probably be broken up into several taxonomic units.

    a. *barbatu.* Creeks and small rivers, Colorado and Arizona. Emerges February–May.

    b. *californica.* Small creeks, California and Arizona.

    c. *cheama.* Large rivers, Canada and northern Rockies, emerges March–early May. Uncommon.

    d. *coloradensis.* Common in creeks and rivers, Rocky Mountains, emerges March–April.

    e. *confusa.* Common in creeks, Coast, Cascade, and Rocky mountains; emerges February–June.

    f. *cygna.* Creeks; Coast, Cascade and Rocky mountains; emerges February–June. Uncommon.

    g. *decepta.* Small creeks, southern Rockies, Colorado; emerges May.

    h. *fibola.* Arizona, northern Mexico; emerges January–March. Uncommon.

    i. *gracilaria.* Widespread and abundant in creeks and small rivers; emerges January–May.

    j. *lineata.* Northern Idaho; emerges March–April. Uncommon.

    k. *mana.* Common, cold springs and streams, Coast, Cascade, and Rocky mountains.

    l. *media.* Uncommon.

    m. *petila.* Creeks and rivers; emerges February–May.

    n. *sex-turberculata.* Common in creeks and rivers, especially in Montana; emerges February–April.

    o. *utahensis*

    p. *uintahi.* Uncommon.

    q. *venosa.* Uncommon.

    r. *vern lis.* Abundant in large and medium streams.

    s. *wavmer.* Common in rivers, all over Rocky Mountains; emerges February–April.

    t. *wanica*

    u. *manitobia.* Northeast.

4) Genus *Eucaphopsis.* One species WNA; wings are a dull gray-black when most *capniids* exhibit shiny black wings.

    a. *brevicauda.* Abundant in creeks and rivers; Canadian, northern, central and southern Rocky Mountains; emerges February–July. 4–5mm.

5) Genus *Isocapnia.* Eleven species WNA; Relatively rare; larger size of most species in comparison to other *capniids;* 20mm. all found in large, clean rivers; all have dwarf males, 60 percent size of regular males; males have no wings.

    a. *grandis.* Common in Pacific Northwest; females 20mm.

    b. *crinita.* Common in Rocky Mountains.

    c. *hyalita.* Common in Rocky Mountains, 15–20mm.

    d. *vedderensis.* Very tiny.

6) Genus *Mesocapnia.* Eleven species WNA, NNA; common in northern locales.
    a. *oenone.* Alaska; emerges August–December, September–October heaviest; Northwest 6–10mm.
    b. *projecta.* Some Southwest; emerges early spring.
7) Genus *Nemocapnia.* One species ENA.
    a. *carolina.* Found in large rivers in southern Appalachians; 12–15mm.
8) Genus *Paracapnia.* Three species ANA; most common in the East.
    a. *angulata.* Common in Massachusetts; emerges April; common in streams of all kinds; 12mm.
    b. *opis.* Emerges April; common in streams of all kinds; 12mm.
    c. *oswegaptera.* Uncommon; Colorado to Oregon.
9) Genus *Utacapnia.* Ten species; ANA; mainly western, but some species in Labrador; 15mm.
    a. *distincta.* Common in Rocky Mountains.
    b. *lemoniana.* Common.
    c. *logana.* Common.
    d. *poda.* Common.
    e. *trava.* Common.
    f. *labradora.* The only eastern representative.

The Willows (Tiny Blacks of Summer)

FAMILY LEUCTRIDAE

The adults of this family are usually small and dark gray or black. Wings are uniformly dark and curl on the sides, which gives a rolled appearance. The nymphs are lightly colored and wing pads are parallel to body axis. Similar to Capniidae, but much more elongated. The emergence is from spring to fall depending on species. Often found in springs or spring creeks.
1) Genus *Despaxia.* One species; WNA; late summer or early fall emergence.
    a. *augusta.* Creeks and small streams; Coast, Cascade, Rocky, and Sierra Nevada mountains; uncommon.
2) Genus *Leuctra.* ENA; Twenty-one species; 6–8mm; long and skinny.
    a. *decepta.* Emerge May–August; relatively uncommon; associated with debris.
    b. *hamula.* Same as *decepta.*
    c. *harfi.* Same as *decepta.*
    d. *sibleyi.* Same as *decepta.*
    e. *tenuis.* Same as *decepta.*
    f. *carolinius.* Same as *decepta.*
3) Genus *Moselia.* One species; Pacific Northwest.
    a. *infuscata.* Abundant PNA; 6–8mm.

4) Genus *Megaleuctra.* Five species; ANA, two species in Rocky Mountains; uncommon, the rest are in Pacific Northwest and Appalachians; over 20mm, brown instead of black.

    a. *kincaidia.* Northern Rocky Mountains; emerges April–July; uncommon.

    b. *stigmata.* Northwest NA; restricted to small springs; only found in spring-fed seeps; uncommon.

5) Genus *Paraleuctra.* Seven species ANA; common in Rocky Mountains. Emerge spring and summer; most common in spring-fed streams.

    a. *forcipata.* Very rapid creeks; Coast, Cascade, Rocky, and Sierra Nevada mountains; emerges April–July.

    b. *jewetti.* Fast, cold creeks; northern, central and southern Rocky Mountains; emerges late May–early June.

    c. *occidentalis.* Creeks and rivers; Coast, Cascade, Rocky, and Sierra Nevada mountains; emerges February–August; most common western species.

    d. *purcelluna.* Rocky Mountains; creeks; emerges May–August; uncommon.

    e. *rickeri.* Fast cold creeks; Rocky Mountains and Alaska; emerges March–July.

    f. *vershina.* This is an abundant species found in both creeks and rivers; Coast, Cascade, Rocky, and Sierra Nevada mountains; emerges March–August; most common western species.

    g. *sara.* Only eastern species.

6) Genus *Perlomyia.* Seven species; ANA; only genus found in large springs in the Rocky Mountains; emerges early spring.

    a. *collaris.* Common in creeks and rivers of Pacific Northwest, Coast, Cascade, Rocky mountains; emerges February–April.

    b. *utahensis.* Common in springs, but found in creeks and small rivers; Coast, Cascade, and Rocky mountains; emerges April–July.

7) Genus *Zealeuctra.* Eight species; ENA; found in permanent streams of all sizes; associated with debris, relatively uncommon; emerges May–August.

    a. *classeni.* Most common East.

    b. *narfi.* Michigan, Wisconsin; most common species; the great yellow and browns.

The Roachlike Tiny Browns of Spring

FAMILY PELTOPERLIDAE

Looks like cockroach; 5–9mm; small brown; adults are small and stout, nymphs are dark brown.

1) Genus *Peltoperla.* Five species; ENA.
   a. *maria.* Common in East; light brown; 10mm; body and head are short; found in small, spring-fed mountain streams only.
2) Genus *Sierraperla.* One species; PNA; uncommon; brown.
3) Genus *Soliperla.* Four species; PNA; uncommon; brown.
4) Genus *Viehoperla.* One species; Southeast; yellow.
5) Genus *Yaraperla.* Two species; WNA.
   a. *Brevis.* Coast, Cascade, Rocky, Sierra Nevada mountains; in spring creeks; 8mm; dark-brown abdomen; found in springs and small rivers; emerges April–August.
   b. *marlana.* Pacific Northwest; British Columbia, uncommon.

The Giant Dark Stones—The Salmon Flies

FAMILY PTERONARCYIDAE

Large dark stoneflies differ from other families in the heavy venation of the anal lobes in the wings. Nymphal gills are in the tufts on thorax and basal abdominal segments.

1) Genus *Pteronarcella.* Two species western North America; 18–20mm; these are the smaller members of the family; 60 percent of other genera.
   a. *badia.* Rocky Mountains and Alaska; common in creeks and rivers below 8,500 feet; distribution parallels *P. californica;* two-year life cycle; emerges May–July.
   b. *regularis.* Northern Rocky Mountains; common in creeks and small rivers in Pacific Northwest; emerges April–June (July 6 on Bitterroot River in Montana); late-afternoon egg laying; 15–16mm; underbody beige gray.
2) Genus *Pteronarcys.* Four species; PNA; these are the largest genera in North America; two species found in Rocky Mountains; dark brown with yellow to salmon-red intersegmental markings.
   a. *californica.* Widespread West; under rocks with accumulation of debris or in beds of aquatic plants; 3–4 year life cycle; emerges mid-April–early August; found mainly in big water.
   b. *dorsata.* Eastern North America and northern part of western North America; most common in rivers of central eastern states; nymphs live in detritus below stony riffles; *nobilis* is a synonymn; found mainly in big water but similar streams can have good populations.
   c. *princeps.* Western; common in creeks and rivers of California and Pacific Northwest, but rare in Rocky Mountains; emerges April–June; found in very small streams only.
   d. *pictetii.* Midwestern; found in big water; emerges late May.

3) Genus *Allonarcys.* Four species ENA; not found in Rocky Mountains; occupies same niche as *Pteronarcys* in West.
     a. *proteus.* Appalachia.
     b. *bilobota.* Appalachia.
     c. *scoti.* Smokies.
     d. *comstocki.* Northeastern Virginia; North.

The Medium Browns

FAMILY PERLODIDAE

subfamily A) *Isoperlinae.* Yellow or brownish and smaller than *Perlodinae.*
     B) *Perlodinae.* Larger than *Isoperlinae.*

 Subfamily *Perlodinae.* Nineteen genera; nymphs are dark with light dorsal pattern; adults are dark brown or black, with bright yellow to orange markings on head and pronotum; the ventral is light in color.
 Subfamily *Isoperlinae.* Three genera; adults are yellow or brown and smaller than *Perlodinae;* nymphs are brightly striped, yellow and brown; *Isoperla* only genus in Rocky Mountains.

Subfamily Perlodinae

1) Genus *Arcynopteryx.* One species; NNA; found only at high elevations.
     a. *compacta.* Common in lakes with rocky shorelines; transcontinental in arctic regions; the common large *Perlodid* in far northern areas; emerges March–May; found in one arm of Lake Superior; 20mm.
2) Genus *Chernokrilus.* Three species; Pacific Northwest; uncommon.
3) Genus *Cultus.* Four species; ANA; small to medium, yellow, lacking gills.
     a. *aestivalis.* Coast, Cascade, Rocky mountains; common in creeks and rivers of the Yellowstone area; emerges April–August.
     b. *pilatus.* Pacific Northwest.
     c. *tostonus.* Coast, Cascade, Rocky, Sierra Nevada mountains; in creeks and rivers; emerges April–August.
     d. *descious.* East; uncommon.
4) Genus *Diploperla.* Two species; ENA.
     a. *robusts.* Uncommon.
     b. *viloba.* Uncommon.
5) Genus *Diura.* Two species; ANA; NNA; medium size; light brown.
     a. *knowltoni.* Coast, Cascade, Rocky, Sierra Nevada mountains; uncommon; nymphs are brightly colored with brown and yellow stripes; emerges April–June.

6) Genus *Helopicus*. Two species; ENA; Midwest; common.
   a. *subvaria*. Important and most common; 20mm.
   b. *galtus*. Uncommon.
7) Genus *Hydroperla*. Two species; ENA.
   a. *cosbyi*. Southern Midwest; 20mm.
   b. *varians*
8) Genus *Isogenoides*. Nine species; ANA; NNA; found in big rivers; 20–25mm; dark brown.
   a. *colubrinus*. Coast, Cascade, Rocky mountains in large rivers; emerges March–August.
   b. *elongatus*. Coast, Cascade, Rocky mountains in large creeks and rivers; common; emerges May–July.
   c. *zionensis*. Rocky Mountains and Alaska; fairly uncommon; emerges May–June.
   d. *decisus*
   e. *doratus*
   f. *frontalis*. West and East.
   g. *krumholzi*. West and Midwest; common.
   h. *nalatus*
   i. *olivaceus*
   j. *subvarians*
   k. *varians*
   l. *hudsonicus*. East; important and common.
9) Genus *Kogatus*. Three species; WNA; small to medium size; vary from yellow to light brown.
   a. *modestus*. Coast, Cascade, Rocky mountains; common in creeks and rivers; emerges August (fall); only common species.
   b. *nonus*. Coast, Cascade, Rocky mountains in creeks and rivers; emerges April–September.
10) Genus *malirekus*. Five species; ENA.
   a. *hastatus*. Pennsylvania and Kentucky; dark brown; 20–25mm.
11) Genus *Megarcys*. The three western species are large, light-brown stoneflies; four species.
   a. *signata*. Coast, Cascade, Rocky mountains; in creeks and rivers; emerges April–August; most common.
   b. *subruncata*. Coast, Cascade, Rocky mountains; in creeks and rivers; emerges April–July.
   c. *watertoni*. Rocky Mountains in fast creeks; emerges April–August; common in Montana.
12) Genus *Oroperla*. One species; PNA; uncommon.
13) Genus *Osopenus*. One species; PNA; uncommon.
14) Genus *Perlinudes*. One species; WNA; uncommon.
15) Genus *Pictetiella*. One species; large, light-brown individuals; uncommon.
16) Genus *Remenus*. One species; ENA; uncommon.
17) Genus *Setvena*. One species; WNA; nymphs are stout and look like large *Isoperla*; uncommon.

18) Genus *Skwala.* Two species; WNA; Coast, Cascade, Rocky, Sierra Nevada mountains; common in creeks and rivers; emerges February–July.
   a. *parallela.* Found in Montana after the ice has gone out; 20mm; black with light abdomen.

Subfamily Isoperlinae

1) Genus *Calliperla.* One species; Pacific Northwest; uncommon.
2) Genus *Isoperla.* Adults are yellow to light brown and are smaller than *Perlodinae;* fifty species; PNA; 13–15mm; very widespread genus.
   a. *bilineata.* Eastern and central North America and southern Rocky Mountains; 1/2-inch yellow Sally; very common in large rivers in East and Midwest; 15mm.
   b. *ebria.* Coast, Cascade, Rocky, Sierra Nevada mountains in creeks and rivers; emerges May–July; dark black in West.
   c. *fulva.* Coast, Cascade, Rocky, Sierra Nevada mountains; common in creeks and rivers; emerges April–August; 15mm, brown.
   d. *fusca.* Coast, Cascade, Rocky mountains; common in creeks; emerges May–August; dark brown; 12mm.
   e. *longiseta.* Great Plains to Rocky Mountains in large rivers; emerges May–mid-July; 10–12mm; small, frail, gray wings with light-brown body.
   f. *mormona.* Coast, Cascade, Rocky, Sierra Nevada mountains in creeks and rivers; emerges May–August; appearance same as *longiseta* but with red abdomen; 11mm; this is the famous Morman Girl.
   g. *patricia.* Coast, Cascade, Rocky, Sierra Nevada mountains; abundant in creeks and rivers; emerges April–August; appearance same as *longiseta* but with red abdomen.
   h. *petersoni.* Alaska and Rocky Mountains; rare; spring creeks; emerges May–November; 12–15mm.
   i. *phalerata.* Coast, Cascade, Rocky mountains; emerges April–August; uncommon.
   j. *pinta.* Coast, Cascade, Rocky mountains in creeks and rivers; Pacific Northwest; emerges March–July; uncommon.
   k. *quinguepunctata.* Coast, Sierra Nevada, Rocky mountains; emerges May–July; red abdomen; 15–17mm; common in some streams in the Rocky Mountains.
   l. *sordida.* Coast, Cascade, Rocky, Sierra Nevada mountains; emerges June–September; dark brown.
   m. *trictura.* Coast, Cascade, Rocky mountains; emerges April–July; uncommon.
   n. *clio.* Wid variety of streams, all ecotypes; emerges May–July; common in East and Midwest; dark brown to black.
   o. *confusa.* Same as *clio.*
   p. *conspicua.* Found in a wide variety of streams; all ecotypes; emerges May–July.

q. *decepta.* Same as *conspicua.*

r. *minima.* Same as *conspicua.*

s. *mohri.* Same as *conspicua.*

t. *richardson.* Same as *conspicua.*

u. *cotta.* Same as *conspicua.*

v. *dicala.* Same as *conspicua.*

w. *emarginata.* Same as *conspicua.*

x. *lata.* Same as *conspicua* .

y. *marlynia.* Same as *conspicua.*

z. *maxima.* Same as *conspicua.*

aa. *minuta.* Common in Midwest; 10mm.

bb. *montana*

cc. *orata*

dd. *signata*

ee. *slossae*

ff. *transmaria.* Common in Midwest; 12–15mm; light-brown, yellow abdomen; wings are light brown.

gg. *truncata*

3) Genus *Rickera.* One species; PNA.

a. uncommon

The Big Goldens

FAMILY PERLIDAE

Distinct because they lack abdominal gills, but possessing profusely branched thoracic gills, this family has two subfamilies, *Acroneuriinae* and *Perlinae.* The former includes most of the western species, the latter the eastern species.

Subfamily Acroneuriinae

1) Genus *Acroneuria.* Twelve species; PNA; eleven species in North America; only one species, *abnormis,* is found in the West and is also found in the East; two-year life cycle; found in fast, well-oxygenated water; emerge May–June.

a. *abnormis.* Eastern and central U.S. and Canada, Montana, Utah, Wyoming, Colorado, Idaho; have been incorrectly called *Calineuria californica* and *Doroneuria theodora* in the past; 1½ inches.

b. *melu*

c. *carolinensis.* #8 Great Brown Stone.

d. *arida*

e. *evalouta*

2) Genus *Attaneuria.* One species; ENA.

a. *ruralis.* Midsummer Yellowlegged Stone; very dark brown.

3) Genus *Beloneuria.* One species; Southeast.
    a. *xanthenas.* Common.
4) Genus *Calineuria.* One species; WNA; Pacific Coast and northern Rocky Mountains; this is the most abundant species in the Pacific Northwest; emerges April–July; Golden Stone.
    a. *californica.* used to be called *Acroneuria californica.*
5) Genus *Doroneuria.* Two species; WNA.
    a. *baumanni.* Canada, northern and central Rocky Mountains; most common near Pacific Coast, lower Columbia River; emerges May–October; dark brown; $1\frac{1}{2}$ inches.
    b. *theodora.* Northern part of Intermountain West; headwaters of the Columbia River; emerges June–September.
6) Genus *Hesperoperla.* One species; WNA; common from Alaska to New Mexico.
    a. *pacifica.* WNA; this is the most widely distributed species of stonefly in the Rocky Mountains; exhibits a wide variety of size, color, and wing length; emerges April–October; important and most common; light brown; $1\frac{1}{2}$ inches.
7) Genus *Perlesta.* Two species; PNA; nymphs have a characteristic freckled appearance; most eastern; genus needs revision.
    a. *placida.* Eastern, central, northern and southern Rocky Mountains; most common in eastern North America; emerges June–August; 12mm; greenish gray; some populations have yellow fringe on outer part of wing.
8) Genus *Perlinella.* Three species; ENA; uncommon; found in gravel riffles of medium and large streams; uncommon in Midwest.
    a. *drymo.* Most common of species; $1\frac{1}{2}$ inches; skinny.

Subfamily Perlinae

1) Genus *Neoperla.* Two species; PNA, common in east with some population in Arizona and New Mexico.
    a. *clymene.* Probably several species are clumped together under *N. clymene*; common in Northeast and as far south as Georgia; rare in Rocky Mountains but present; emerges June–September; most common in Midwest; also found in East; 12mm; light brown.
2) Genus *Claassenia.* One species; WNA; East in Canada to Hudson Bay.
    a. *sabulosa.* A top carnivore and very active nymph; 32mm long; emerges June–September; used to be called *arfita;* black wings, yellow-and-orange abdomen; males have almost no wings.
3) Genus *Pargnetina.* Five species; ENA; two-year life cycle; found in rocks in fast streams; emerges June–July.
    a. *media.* Emerges June–July; Midwest; common.
    b. *imarginata.* East; common.

4) Genus *Phasganophora.* Two species; ENA.
    a. *capitata.* #8 Great Eastern Stone; found in rocks in fast water of medium and large streams; very common in East.

The Delicate Greens and Yellows

FAMILY CHLOROPERLIDAE

Adults can be distinguished by reduced wing venation, oval pronotum, and delicate yellow, green, or olive color. The one genus in the family *(Utaperla)* is dark, similar to *Capnia.* Forking in the second anal vein of the forewing easily separates the families. The nymphs exhibit a complete absence of external gills.

1) Genus *Alloperla.* Seventeen species; ANA; adults of all species are bright green, except for *A. delicata,* which is yellow.
    a. *delicata.* Coast, Cascade, Rocky, Sierra Nevada mountains; abundant in creeks and small rivers in the Pacific Northwest; emerges April–August; yellow; 10–12mm.
    b. *medueda.* Coast, Cascade, Rocky mountains; found in creeks and small rivers; emerges April–August; green; common in northern Rocky Mountains.
    c. *pilosa.* At high elevations only in Colorado; in small creeks; emerges June–July.
    d. *serrata.* Coast, Cascade, Rocky mountains; creeks; emerges April–August; common and important.
    e. *severa.* Coast, Cascade, Rocky mountains, Alaska; common in small creeks; emerges May–September; most common in Rocky Mountains.
    f. *caudata.* Ozark Mountains.
    g. *atlantica.* Most common in East.
    h. *leonarda.* Common in northern Midwest, Michigan.
2) Genus *Hastaperla.* Three species; ANA.
    a. *brevis.* Common in streams of all sizes; emerges June–July; yellow; very common; 6–8mm; common in the East.
    b. *orpha.* Common in streams of all sizes; emerges June–July; uncommon in Midwest.
    c. *pacifica.* Common and widespread; emerges August.
3) Genus *Neariperla.* One species; WNA; yellow adults.
    a. *forcipata.* Coast, Cascade, Rocky mountains; in creeks and small rivers; emerges July–September; uncommon.
4) Genus *Rasvena.* One species; ENA; uncommon.
    a. *terna*
5) Genus *Suwallia.* Four species; ANA; 8mm; delicate yellow.
    a. *autumna.* Coast, Cascade, Rocky mountains in small rivers and creeks; emerges June–October.

b. *lineosa.* Coast, Cascade, Rocky Mountains in small rivers and creeks; emerges May–September; most common and important.

c. *pallidula.* Coast, Cascade, Rocky, Sierra Nevada mountains; most common and widespread members of the family in the Rocky Mountains; emerges May–October; most common and important.

d. *marganita.* East and Northeast.

6) Genus *Swelta.* Twenty-three species; 10–12mm; yellow to yellow-brown.

a. *albertensis.* Common; emerges May–August.

b. *borealis.* Coast, Cascade, Rocky, Sierra Nevada mountains; common.

c. *coloradensis.* Coast, Cascade, Rocky, Sierra Nevada mountains; common; emerges April–August.

d. *fidelis.* Coast, Cascade, Rocky, Sierra Nevada mountains; abundant in creeks and rivers in the Pacific Northwest; emerges May–September.

e. *gaufini.* Utah and Idaho.

f. *lamba.* Coast, Cascade, Rocky mountains; common in spring; emerges June–October.

g. *revelstoka.* Coast, Cascade, Rocky mountains; common in fast streams and cold lakes in high elevations; emerges July–August.

h. *omkos.* Northeast; important and most common.

i. *medina.* South.

j. *lateralis.* South.

7) Genus *Triznaka.* Three species; WNA; 8mm.

a. *diversa.* Coast, Cascade, Rocky, Sierra Nevada mountains; common in creeks and small rivers; emerges May–July; frail yellow, no markings.

b. *pintada.* Creeks and small rivers; emerges May–August; dark marking with yellow background.

c. *signata.* Coast, Cascade, Rocky mountains in creeks and small rivers; emerges May–August; dark markings with yellow background.

8) Genus *Kathroperla.* One species; WNA; 20–25mm (much larger than the rest of the family); dark brown.

a. *perdita.* Coast, Cascade, Rocky mountains; creeks and small rivers; emerges May–July.

9) Genus *Paraperla.* Two species; WNA; 11–17mm; darkly colored; dark brown.

a. *frontalis.* Coast, Cascade, Rocky, Sierra Nevada mountains in creeks, small rivers and cold lakes; emerges April–August.
frontalis. Coast, Cascade, Rocky, Sierra Nevada mountains in creeks, small rivers and cold lakes; emerges April–August.

b. *wilsoni.* Coast, Cascade, Rocky mountains in creeks and small rivers; emerges March–August.

10) Genus *Utaperla*. Two species; ANA; adults are black; 10mm or less.
    a. *sopladora*. Coast, Cascade, Rocky mountains; emerges May–July; high-mountain habitat.
    b. *gaspaciana*. Quebec and eastern U.S.; uncommon.

Bibliography

BAUMANN, RICHARD W., GAUFIN, ARDEN, R., SURDICK, REBECCA F. *The Stoneflies (Plecoptera) of The Rocky Mountains.* The American Entomological Society at the Academy of Natural Sciences. Philadelphia, 1977.

BROOKS, CHARLES. *Nymph Fishing for Larger Trout.* Crown Publishers, Inc., New York, 1976.

FRISCON, THEODORE H. *The Stoneflies, or Plecoptera of Illinois.* Entomological Reprint Specialists. Urbana, Illinois, 1935.

HITCHCOCK, STEPHEN W. *Guide to the Insects of Connecticut, Part VII. The Plecoptera or Stoneflies of Connecticut.* State Geological and Natural History Survey of Connecticut; Department of Environmental Protection, Bulletin 107, 1974.

Poul Jorgensen's Modern Trout Flies and how to tie them. Nick Lyons Books/Doubleday. New York, 1979.

MERRITT, RICHARD W. AND CUMMINS, KENNETH W. *An Introduction to the Aquatic Insects of North America.* Kendall/Hunt Publishing Co. Dubuque, 1978.

SCHWIEBERT, ERNEST. *Nymphs.* Winchester Press. New York, 1973.

USINGER, ROBERT L. *Aquatic Insects of California.* University of California Press. Berkeley, 1968.

Index